FAITH IN EXETER

FAITH IN EXETER

THE STORY OF THE

PALACE GATE PROJECT

TREVOR GARDNER

with

RICHARD FROST

Foreword by
Revd Dr Leslie Griffiths

Published by Palace Gate Project
3 Palace Gate, Exeter EX1 1JA

A Project of
Exeter Community Umbrella Ltd
(Registered Charity No. 1026229)

© Palace Gate Project 1996

All rights reserved. No part of this book may be reproduced
or transmitted in any form or by any means,
electronic or mechanical, including photocopying,
recording, or by information storage and retrieval system,
without permission in writing from the publisher.

ISBN 0 9527701 0 5

Cover design by Nick Jones
Photograph by Christopher Wilberforce
Printed by St Michael's Press, Exeter

CONTENTS

Acknowledgments	1
Foreword	3
1 New Wine from the Warehouse	5
2 Food, Furniture & Funding	14
3 Homelessness: A Local View	25
4 Hands On, Hands Together	36
5 The Voucher Scheme	49
6 The Soup Kitchen & Christmas Care	52
7 The Drop-In Service	59
8 The Counselling Service	66
9 The Turntable Furniture Project	71
10 The St Petrock's Day Centre	76
11 Influencing the Influential	91
12 Thoughts of a "Holy Helper"	95
13 The Way Ahead	101
Appendix 1 Aims of The Palace Gate Project	111
Appendix 2 The St Petrock's Judgment	112
Appendix 3 Exeter Community Umbrella	115
Appendix 4 Addresses	118

ACKNOWLEDGMENTS

For those of us who have been involved, the past six years have been remarkable, from the initial discussions about possible development of Exeter's Palace Gate Centre to the opening of the Day Centre at St Petrock's Church - and there is still work to be done in the heart of the city. So it is good to see this book in print, putting on record the remarkable achievements of Trevor Gardner and others.

So many people have been involved in the Palace Gate Project from the beginning that it is invidious to single out any for acknowledgment. The members of the first working party should be thanked for their vision and hard work, and the subsequent committee members have all given much time to implementing the vision. The people at South Street Baptist Church have shown much patience and forbearance at times. Alongside Trevor, there have been numerous volunteers, only a few of whom are named in the text.

In the production of this fascinating book, particular thanks are due to Peter Cousins who collated information and wrote a first draft. This has been worked on by Richard Frost, who has collaborated with Trevor to produce this final version. I hope that all who read this book will glimpse something of the excitement of the Project, and of the commitment and hard work of all involved in it.

Revd Michael Selman
Chair, Palace Gate Project Management Committee
Exeter April 1996

FOREWORD

I visited Exeter while I was President of the Methodist Conference and heard about the innovative work being done. I've built up a picture of the plight of homeless people across the land. I've worked closely with Shelter and other organisations and have recognised the various faces and facets of homelessness, a phenomenon that challenges our understanding of human rights and natural justice in the most radical way. What I particularly appreciated in the narrative that follows is the reminder that homelessness is not just a problem in London. It occurs again and again in pretty and historic cities like Exeter, thus challenging the idyllic picture that most of us form of such places. I can corroborate this important corrective point from experiences gained in other towns. This book also reminds us of the wide variety of personal circumstances that lead to homelessness. It challenges the stigmatising and stereotyping of homeless people as if they were all guilty for their own plight and deserving nothing but our contempt. The final thing I've appreciated in reading this account has been the way Christian compassion and fellow feeling have once again responded in the most practical way to human need and marginalised people.

Please read, mark and inwardly digest the truths that Trevor Gardner and Richard Frost have laid before us. I hope this book stimulates greater interest and strengthens commitment to fighting this social injustice in the name of Christ, our incarnate Lord and our redeemer.

Revd Dr Leslie Griffiths MA
President of the Methodist Conference 1994/95

CHAPTER ONE

NEW WINE FROM THE WAREHOUSE

"Room at the Inn for the Homeless"
It made a good headline in Exeter's *Express & Echo* newspaper on 24 December 1994. The High Street shops were full to overflowing and there was little space on the crowded pavements. There could not have been a more appropriate time than Christmas for a city centre church to open its doors to homeless people.

According to the opinion polls, most people think of Exeter as a good place to live. Very few, one suspects, would associate the city with poverty or homelessness. This book tells the story of how the people of Exeter became aware that these were everyday realities in their historic city and how they did something about it.

From one point of view, it's not a sensational success story. There was no one visionary person who assessed the needs, master-minded a scheme to meet them, and finally supervised its execution. There was no master plan, no grand design. But there was willingness and commitment and that, as it turned out, was what mattered.

Looked at rather differently, the story depicts an amazing success. It's about how a small shoot can grow into a tree. About how members from different churches joined forces to meet a local need. About a city that responded to a challenge of which it had been only dimly aware. About cooperation between churches, official agencies and individuals.

These first two chapters of our story look at the history of the Palace Gate Centre and how that developed to become the inter-church Palace Gate

Project. Homelessness was, and remains, an important concern of the Project, thus chapters three and four offer insights into the situation that affects homeless people. From this historical, practical and theoretical base have grown several individual projects and a campaigning role. Each of these aspects has its own chapter and we hope they will be of particular use and interest to others who wish to respond to homelessness in their own town or city. The book ends with some further reflections and a look ahead.

A city-centre church

The opening of the St Petrock's Day Centre on Christmas Eve, 1994, was the result of an ecumenical effort: but its roots lay in what had happened in just one Exeter church between 1976 and 1991.

South Street Baptist Church was founded in the early 1650s. It has been on its present site in South Street since 1775 and the worship centre was built in 1825. South Street itself is on the edge of Exeter's historical West Quarter, which in pre-Second World War days was a poverty-stricken area of narrow streets running down to the River Exe and the Quay, where ships that had come up the Ship Canal unloaded their cargoes. Alongside its preaching and worship, its conversions and baptisms, South Street Baptist Church also had a tradition of good works and social concern.

During the 1970s the church members realised that changing circumstances were demanding a response: people were moving out of central Exeter, so should the church relocate nearer to the outskirts and the new housing estates? Alternatively, should it merge with another free church congregation? Or, if it stayed put, what should be its role?

The then minister, the Reverend Brian Haymes, posed the question, 'What does it mean to be the people of God as a church in the city centre?' After some serious thought the church settled for two priorities: worship and service.

They looked hard at what was happening in South Street and the High Street. They observed that during the day there were a number of elderly people with little apparent purpose in life, shoppers and tourists, and unemployed people with no paid work and nowhere to go. And then at night, there were young people, voluntary groups meeting and caring organisations on the look-out for people in need.

The members of South Street Baptist Church believed they ought to serve as a Christian presence in this setting. They realised that getting alongside people in this way would be rather different from meeting folk who were willing to attend a service once or twice on Sunday. Although at the time, they didn't realise the extent of the difference.

They didn't target any particular areas of need but committed themselves as a church to being available and vulnerable. They also agreed that the main purpose would not be to make converts.

New vision, new building

The premises, however, presented a serious problem. The building was of traditional Baptist church design with pews, galleries and a high pulpit, and as such was not suitable for social interaction. There was also a church hall, around the corner in Palace Gate, but the layout was less than ideal: a large hall, with a few ancillary rooms.

In spite of the difficulties, several activities were started. A Friendship Club for elderly people met one day each week, serving hot meals. Two mornings per week there was a playgroup for under-5s. The minister ran a "listening ear" advice centre on a weekday evening. And once a week, a lunch was provided for people who wanted to come and listen to a short address followed by discussion. All these services functioned well, which encouraged the church to plan future developments. However it was becoming clear that the church hall was unsuitable, not least because it was not on the same site as the church itself. The Christian caring seemed to have been separated from the worshipping congregation.

When Jesus stood still

Brian Haymes moved on and when the Reverend John Stroud first visited South Street Baptist Church in 1977, his sights were fixed several thousand miles west on a hospital chaplaincy in the USA. But before taking a final decision he asked the Baptist Union (the Church's governing body) if there was a church somewhere that he and his wife should consider.

He found that this more or less normal Baptist church building possessed one remarkable feature: at the back of it, in Palace Gate, was a wine warehouse and bottling factory which the church had bought one year previously.

During the late 18th and early 19th centuries William Kennaway had developed a thriving business by exporting woollen cloth and bringing back claret, port and Madeira up the Ship Canal to the Quay and then through the West Quarter to the premises in Palace Gate. Competition from 20th century supermarkets and off-licences had ruined the Kennaway business with the result that South Street Baptist Church had found itself challenged by the possibility of buying the building.

With superb faith the congregation agreed to sell the church hall and buy the warehouse. As it happened, the Shilhay Community wanted to expand its provision for homeless people and many people thought it fitting that the church hall should become a haven for them. So, the old hall was bought by

Devon County Council for the Shilhay Community, who continue to run it as a direct access hostel for up to thirty homeless men.

So it was that the church secretary, the late Bernard Shorland, led John Stroud into a wilderness of dust, cobwebs and empty bottles behind the church. As he did so, Bernard expressed his vision, 'Here in this corner, for example,' he enthused, 'we shall have the kitchen. And here will be a room for people to meet in.'

Bernard's enthusiasm changed the pattern of the Stroud family's life for almost twenty years. John Stroud committed himself to the new venture and later was to serve as chair of the Palace Gate Project management committee during its first two years.

For John Stroud, one gospel story (Mark 10:46-52) illuminates the significance of what is now called the Palace Gate Centre. When the blind beggar, Bartimaeus, called out to Jesus, a crowd of Jesus' supporters were very upset about the disturbance. As they tried to silence Bartimaeus and he insisted on being heard, so he took centre stage. Jesus alone responded positively. On his way to Jerusalem where the cross of crucifixion awaited him, Jesus saw Bartimaeus in need: and he stopped.

These gospel incidents sometimes transform themselves into icons. 'Is it possible to see the cross itself,' John Stroud asks, 'as God "stopping" for his creation? And must not the church learn to "stop" and respond in this way?' Jesus didn't decide what Bartimaeus needed: he asked him what he wanted. The projects that grew from the Kennaway warehouse can all be seen in this light.

Opening up the walls

Buying the Kennaway warehouse was one thing, putting it to use quite another. Dirty and derelict, it was also the only place available for all the activities that had gone on in the hall which South Street Baptist Church had sold. Refurbishing was too urgent to be left to the DIY enthusiasts in the congregation.

The work entailed making the ground floor fit for use; opening up the walls and fitting glass doors so that the church building and the warehouse could be clearly seen to be one; renaming the altered church building the "Worship Area" which continued to accommodate the baptistry, a cross and an open Bible. But the Worship Area would become multi-purpose, available for use by playgroups, luncheon clubs or barn dances. Symbolically, the front gates of the church which separated the building from South Street itself were removed and the entrance to the building remodelled.

All this called for money and labour. From the nearby Anglican church in St Leonard's parish came a newly retired fund-raiser who offered his services for six months and did wonders in raising money, largely from local sources. The final cost was £250,000 - a lot of money for a church to raise even today and a very great deal in 1979!

As for the labour, much of this was provided in a way that was to become more and more common in future years as the Palace Gate Centre generated the Palace Gate Project. Unemployment being a matter of concern to the government, funds were available to agencies which could provide jobs. Government funding was secured for a project which would without any doubt benefit the community as a whole.

An open door

The doors of the Palace Gate Centre were formally opened in Summer 1979 by Sir Peter Mills, a then local MP who was also Chairman of the Christian Fellowship of the House of Commons. For some, the ceremony may have seemed like the successful achievement of a visionary design. In truth, it was the beginning of a new venture into the unknown.

The new Centre was used to serve the local community in all sorts of ways. The Friendship Club continued to supply hot lunches, with eighty meals served every Friday. The playgroup also continued, at first on three mornings each week, later on four; in addition, a Parent and Toddler Group was started. A new development was the Coffee Shop, serving light meals every Thursday, later extended to Tuesdays as well. One customer described it as 'The only restaurant in Exeter where you could sit for four hours without being asked to order anything.' The Coffee Shop could be seen to be Christian: glass doors led from it into the Worship Area, posters in the hall presented the Christian message, and a church representative was also present. But the volunteer staff were careful not to invade privacy or proselytise. There was also a Day Centre for elderly people, arranged jointly with Social Services. This ran every weekday and catered for about fifty people.

All this made considerable demands on the congregation of about 130 people. John Stroud commented in a video made for the Baptist Home Mission Fund that one of the most encouraging things about the Palace Gate Centre was the way it had shown that ordinary church members could function usefully in all sorts of ways without extended training.

The Baptist Home Mission Fund became involved when it decided to support the work of the Centre financially and to allocate to the church a second minister, at that time the Reverend Ralph Drake, as chaplain to the

Centre. It also financed a social worker for two years. Other Exeter churches also benefited from their help and advice.

The accommodation was a boon to local voluntary organisations. The Exeter Deaf Club had been meeting in Social Service premises nearby. When local government reorganisation resulted in their needing to find a new venue they met at the Centre on three evenings each week. The Blind Club also used the Centre for its quarterly meetings and for occasional social functions. Because there were no steps on the ground floor, the Centre was ideal for meetings of people with mobility problems. The Exeter branch of Cruse needed more space and after moving to the Centre attendance at their monthly meetings rose from forty to one hundred.

There were other voluntary groups too, twenty or more altogether, so the Centre had no difficulty in achieving the high plant utilization which is demanded by secular management but which also makes sense in terms of Christian stewardship.

New facilities - new problems

All the same, there were problems. One was the categories of people using the facilities. Many of them had needs which could not readily be met. They sometimes behaved in ways which were not at all what church members were accustomed to! To exclude them was out of the question, so long as they were not heavily disruptive. Exeter was suffering from the chronic social and economic diseases of the 1980s and 1990s: homelessness, unemployment and the poverty trap - these people needed compassion not exclusion.

By 1990, changes in the community were making it increasingly clear that new needs were demanding attention. These changes corresponded to national developments: a changing world, a changing culture. As psychiatric hospitals were closed, so former patients appeared on the streets. The number of elderly people occupying sheltered accommodation in the city centre was increasing and many were finding it more difficult to obtain day care. At the same time, there were more homeless people. The stress experienced by workers in the business community was becoming more severe. More young people were gravitating to the city centre, attracted by greater entertainment opportunities and lack of structured activities elsewhere.

A second big problem was the increasing burden of staffing and administration. The two were related but different. For even if more volunteers came forward to help with the growing volume of work, this would also add to the responsibilities of "line management" and "the board of directors". Another aspect of administration was the need to work with government agencies, especially in the new situations created by the purchaser/provider culture. This meant that government agencies followed a policy of buying services from a range of private, public and voluntary agencies, of which the Centre was now one.

These were some of the factors that were to lead John Stroud and the Reverend Michael Selman, Rector of the Anglican Parish of Central Exeter, to agree on an approach to the Church Urban Fund for assistance. The Fund's involvement was to mark the beginning of a new phase in the Christian response to social problems in central Exeter.

CHAPTER TWO

FOOD, FURNITURE & FUNDING

The Palace Gate Centre had always been a South Street Baptist Church initiative but with the expanding and increasingly demanding nature of the work, it was natural that the Parish of Central Exeter should become involved.

During the 1980s there was widespread concern about the poverty in Britain's cities and the then Archbishop of Canterbury, now Lord Runcie, set up a commission of enquiry. It was the Archbishop's Commission's task to look into urban deprivation, particularly within the inner cities of Britain. The Commission was to ascertain levels of poverty, marginalisation and need and make recommendations to both Church and nation that could begin to address and respond to them. In 1985, the Archbishop's Commission published its findings in a report entitled, *Faith in the City*.

One development resulting from that report was the establishment of the Church Urban Fund (CUF) to support inner city projects in what became known as Urban Priority Areas (UPAs). This represented a very significant commitment by the Church of England and called upon every parish, whether rural or inner city, to contribute. Each Anglican diocese was also required to assess its own parishes to establish the nature and degree of need. When Michael Selman identified a high level of social deprivation in his parish and described the findings at a meeting of local clergy, John Stroud talked about how South Street Baptist Church had been trying to meet some of the needs.

It was clear that the Central Parish, a UPA, which had been formed by amalgamating what had originally been four separate parishes, faced a challenge similar to that experienced by South Street Baptist Church, although with the added complication, or opportunity, of possessing six church buildings of its own. Concern to see these used responsibly had led the Parochial Church Council (PCC) to reorder the interiors of St Stephen's Church and St Pancras' Church to make them available to community groups for meetings, fund-raising events, coffee mornings, exhibitions and the like.

Applying for funding

During 1990, in order to put together the application to the CUF and plan what was to become the Palace Gate Project, a management committee, under the chairmanship of John Stroud, was brought together from both the Central Parish and South Street Baptist Church. and included people with vision and commitment.

The committee identified three immediate needs. There must be (1) a Community Development Worker (CDW) to operate the Project; (2) a Secretary/Receptionist lest the CDW sink without trace in a mass of paperwork; (3) a Centre Manager/Administrator to organise the Palace Gate Centre, to keep track of its bookings and to oversee the welcome, support and liaison with user groups.

The involvement of the Central Parish not only meant that the work of the Palace Gate Centre was now an ecumenical expression of Christian fellowship, but the partnership inspired a great deal of new thinking as individuals and agencies from the Church of England made their contributions. For example, it was Martyn Goss, Social Responsibility Officer of the Exeter Diocesan Board for Christian Care, who first suggested the need for a CDW. Very practical help was also given by the Central Parish's PCC. As appointments were made, the PCC took up the substantial burden of accounting and financial responsibility - at a time when there was no other local body legally able to do so.

Preparing the CUF application was no easy task. It was necessary to explain what the Palace Gate Centre was already doing and to show that any money given by the CUF would be used effectively and responsibly. In effect, the committee had to present a business plan. Although preparing the submission was tough, the discipline of facing the issues proved to be very helpful. Already those responsible understood the importance of drawing upon as much relevant local experience as possible, consulting in particular with Devon County Council Social Services and agencies concerned with mental health.

Demonstrating to the CUF that the money it made available would be spent efficiently focused attention on the need for new management structures, which had to be both professional and ecumenical. This necessary change obviously brought with it a danger that the new management structures might become distanced from the grassroots. Some Centre workers began to fear that their original clients might suffer. The Baptist tradition of member involvement sat uneasily alongside the new, more professional, management system. The administrative changes resulted in a significant change of style. But the time had come when legal, commercial and statutory involvement were required and the changes were inevitable if the work begun by South Street Baptist Church was to expand.

When they submitted their application at the end of 1990, the committee set a target funding figure of £100,000.

In the event, CUF gave a grant of £40,000 which was to finance the CDW for three years. The Diocesan Board of Finance through its Priority Areas Funding Group granted a further £20,000 over three years, in the first instance for a caterer, though this was later amended to provide continuation funding for the CDW in the fourth and fifth years. The posts for Centre Manager/Administrator and Secretary/Receptionist remained unfilled.

Trevor Gardner

Now the search was on for someone to fill the vital post of Community Development Worker. Advertising in the spring of 1991 brought an encouraging response including applicants with good qualifications and experience. In July 1991, from the short list of six, the Palace Gate Project management committee unanimously selected a candidate whose vision and initiative had made a strong impression: Trevor Gardner.

Trevor grew up in Exeter. He describes himself as a Methodist, 'by accident of birth', and attended the local Methodist church with his parents. Bored by Sunday School, his Christian commitment was later to be deepened through the church youth club. In future years, he realised the immense importance of such clubs in helping young people to gain worthwhile values for living and became a youth leader himself. He went to the local secondary modern school, where he became head boy, and left at the age of 16, having gained three 'O' levels, including English, despite having dyslexia. Trevor feels that he was destined for a very average kind of life. After a year at college, where he gained two 'A' level passes (Engineering Drawing and Geometric Building Drawing) plus 'O' level Maths, he went to work for the Inland Revenue, ignoring the advice of friends and teachers who told him he should become a draughtsman. Later, he trained as a Methodist Local Preacher and for some time considered the ordained ministry.

In 1988 and now married to Janet, Trevor had had enough of the Inland Revenue. Every day he felt more reluctant to face a job that was grinding him down and would, he felt, ultimately destroy him. Jan was even having to kick him out of bed in the morning! In spite of the claims of Jamie, then eighteen months old, Trevor and Jan agreed, after much prayer, heart-searching and loss of sleep, that they would role-reverse. Trevor would become a househusband. Janet worked full time as an occupational therapist and, later, returned home twice daily to breast-feed their second son, Luke, born in 1990.

Trevor learned a lot during those three years as a househusband. Isolated in the home, he experienced at first hand the sense of marginalisation that afflicts so many wives and mothers. He also discovered that looking after the home was much harder work than he had expected. It was, as he says, 'A complex agenda involving about three million different tasks, many of them needing to be done simultaneously!' He now sees it as a good preparation for what was to follow. Trevor also worked as a relief manager at three probation hostels, a voluntary helper for the probation service and campaigned for unisex nappy-changing facilities in Exeter.

There was plenty of time to think during these years, particularly when he took the children for walks along the riverside, and Trevor came to realise that the way forward was not to be an ordained minister, nor to be involved in either social work or the probation service.

Then a friend showed him the advertisement for the job as a Community Development Worker at Palace Gate. The closing date for applications had passed, but all the same Trevor was interested to learn that work of this kind was going on in Exeter and phoned to ask for more information, since he wanted to keep in touch with the work and pray for it. Michael Selman suggested it was not too late to submit an application.

Predictably, Trevor found himself in competition with professionals. At first sight the decision to appoint him might seem surprising since there were better qualified and more experienced candidates. Trevor began low on the list and later said of the appointments panel, 'Either they were crazy people or there was something happening beyond our control.' What prompted the unanimous decision to appoint him? 'His enthusiasm,' said one member of the panel. 'And a sense that he was able to dream dreams and put flesh on them.' In addition, Trevor was a local man, possessing that useful quality of knowledge about the place in which he was to work. But it was his enthusiasm which was to prove to so many that Trevor was the right person for this new role.

Up and running

A commissioning service took place on 12 September 1991 - an occasion which filled South Street Baptist Church and one at which Richard Frost and Trevor met for the first time. Seven weeks later, following the retirement of Ralph Drake, the Reverend Mary Cotes joined the staff of South Street Baptist Church. Mary felt a particular concern for the Project, in which she was to play a significant part.

After Trevor was appointed the work took off very quickly indeed. Within a few weeks the needs of homeless people were identified as a vital concern. Trevor floated an idea which would later become an important reality: might the hungry people on the streets be helped by a system of meal vouchers to be supplied by churches and individuals? The vouchers could be exchanged at the Coffee Shop at the Palace Gate Centre and at other outlets in Exeter.

As well as the Voucher Scheme, within three months of Trevor's appointment, a soup kitchen was up and running. It was clear, even at this early point, that the Palace Gate Project was involved in high risk, demanding work that was not necessarily within the scope or expertise of the average church committee. With great courage and faith and more than a little anxiety, the Project management committee continued to support the work that Trevor was beginning to generate in a professional and sensitive way. They took care that the necessary checks and balances were in place to ensure that nothing was done that was outside their expertise or scope. Yet a soup kitchen was arguably a risky thing for the Project to begin with, not least when it was to be staffed by volunteers. Trevor later compared it to filling a powder keg - an undertaking that, if not well managed, could have exploded with dramatic and devastating consequences. Yet the committee continued to cope, albeit very quickly realising the nature and the demands of the work.

Another idea which gradually developed during these early months of the Project was for a furniture recycling scheme. This would need considerable funding - for renting premises, buying vehicles and employing staff. Once again the committee members responded remarkably as they went through a very steep learning curve. They agreed to consider and undertake setting up what was to become the Turntable Furniture Project and also to serve as its initial management committee.

Yet the organization that had grown so quickly still had no bank account of its own - it was working through those of the South Street Baptist Church and the Central Parish. It did not have charitable status and had no limited liability, a state of affairs which was beginning to cause the committee some anxiety, particularly as now it was taking on more responsibility and risk in undertaking leases with Exeter City Council for the Turntable Furniture Project as well as other duties. And this was still in the days when the St Petrock's Day Centre was still only a glimmer in Trevor's eye. The committee also recognised the need for a new structure and some way in which the work that was being generated by the Palace Gate Project could be released. They had no means or expertise in identifying how this could happen, only the knowledge that it must.

Trevor had conversations with Martyn Goss and Jim Michelmore, a local solicitor, who had recently retired and was willing to help to enable this new work to continue and develop in a way that was professionally and legally sound. It was important to allow the Palace Gate Project to do what it did best - caring for people - and to ensure that the necessary but sometimes laborious aspects such as charitable status and company law should be handled separately. These initial talks led to the setting up of the Exeter Community Umbrella, a limited charitable company, and this provided the mechanisms necessary for the whole Project.

At the same time as the Exeter Community Umbrella was being planned, the Palace Gate Project management committee also felt the need for the Project to become more ecumenical and more representative of all the local churches who had increasingly become involved during the first eighteen months. It also recognised that other gifts, skills and expertise needed to be drawn into the committee so that it could do the professional job of enabling and supporting a work which had become more diverse and complex.

This process was not without problems and there were times when the original committee felt anxious about the degree of responsibility and the volume and complexity of the work that was being generated as the Project took hold and so quickly became accepted and taken seriously throughout the city. In 1993, with great humility, the original committee realised that the Project had outgrown their original vision and expertise and were prepared to step aside in order for the Project to develop into new areas.

In January 1994, a new Palace Gate Project management committee, with Michael Selman as chair, was appointed with representatives from each of the city centre churches. These were "hand picked", since the purpose of broadening the committee was not merely to acquire a representative from each church, possibly people with interest but no expertise, but for each church to provide people who were not only interested but also possessed a skill or gift. Thus one church identified someone with personnel and training expertise, another sent an accountant, another a solicitor and so on. Two or three of the original committee remained to ensure continuity.

At the same time it was also being realised that the Palace Gate Centre, run by South Street Baptist Church, had no management system. The work done by both the Project and the Centre had grown too large and diverse to be managed by one group of people. So it was agreed that a separate Palace Gate Centre Management Committee should also be set up.

It is easy to look back upon those first three years of the Palace Gate Project and see the stress and the tension which was caused by a management system that was designed for something before it commenced. Yet who could ever have dreamt of the way in which the Project would develop and grow - and with such speed! Looking back, it is a credit to the original committee that they were not only willing to accept the challenge of setting up the Project but also that they were wise enough to realise when their expertise and gifts were exhausted. It was a considerable achievement when they decided the time had come to hand the Project over to a more suitable and appropriate body that would ensure fulfilment both for its future development and its ecumenical origins.

More money matters

The money from the Church Urban Fund was designed to be used as pump-priming: if a project is going to be successful and its need confirmed, this will generally be known within the first three years. After this time, it is expected that the local congregations and community should take on the responsibility for continuation funding. In certain circumstances, however, it is possible to return to CUF for a further two years funding.

So much had been achieved in the first three years of the Palace Gate Project and yet, although many churches did donate money, it had been difficult during this time to persuade some local congregations and the wider community to see the worth of the Project in financial terms.

In the event, CUF agreed to fund the Project for a further two years. The level of funding was less than in the initial period and was gained because of partnership funding from another church organisation, the Mission Alongside the Poor Project (MAPP).

MAPP is the Methodist Church's equivalent of CUF and, in 1994, the Palace Gate Project made application to it with the backing of the local Methodist Circuit and District. MAPP funding to the value of £15,000 was made on a diminishing sliding scale over a three year period. This was a greatly welcomed source of funding and provided a real stop-gap as well as a longer-term measure for the Project while waiting for news of the CUF continuation funding. It was also good to receive money from another denomination to show in a very public way the ecumenical nature of the Project.

Over the years, the Project has received one-off and ongoing financial support from many individuals, statutory organisations, churches and charities. Inevitably, there are too many to mention by name, although some will be referred to in the chapters that follow.

Many hundreds of hours have also been spent developing the good practice aspects of the Project's work. For example, policies relating to conditions of employment, confidentiality, security, health and safety, equal opportunities as well as many other areas have been thought through and committed to paper.

Before describing in detail the actual work carried out by the Palace Gate Project and its various "offspring", to which we have already briefly referred, it is important to ask two questions which are central to all that has been embarked upon and achieved:

- What is homelessness?
- Why should the Church care about homeless people?

It is in the next two chapters that we seek to offer some answers.

CHAPTER THREE

HOMELESSNESS: A LOCAL VIEW

Frank was fortunate in having accommodation. Along with his wife, Laura, and their baby, Sam, they spent several months in bed and breakfast accommodation. They were glad to receive food parcels from the Palace Gate Project as they moved from one B&B to another. Then they settled for an attic room up three flights of stairs. There was no bath and Sam's pram had to be carried up and down each day, but they hoped this might help them gain a few more housing points. The walls were thin, there were many other families with screaming babies, little privacy and no facilities for childcare. One Saturday, when Trevor called to deliver a high chair, he found that Frank had hanged himself during the night. The stress had proved too much for him. The coroner's verdict was suicide - the housing crisis was not mentioned. Laura and Sam went back to her mum and family to try and rebuild their lives.

Homelessness has been an increasingly grave problem throughout the 1980s and the 1990s and there is no sign that it is being seriously addressed, let alone abated. It is said that in the United Kingdom 1 in 250 people is homeless - equivalent to more than twice the population of Exeter.

Recent research has thrown further light on the subject. The Churches National Housing Coalition (CNHC) have identified several startling realities about the housing situation in the country as a whole. CNHC make the following points: every working day, more than 1,000 households apply to local councils for help on grounds of homelessness; there are up to 150,000 homeless young people in Britain today; in the past ten years, over 3,000,000 people (half of them children) have been registered as homeless by local authorities. In Spring 1995, a report, from the Joseph Rowntree Foundation Inquiry Group established that the gap between rich and poor in the UK was greater than at any time in the previous fifty years and that income inequality grew more rapidly between 1977 and 1990 than in any other industrialised country except New Zealand. In November 1995, ten years after *Faith in the City*, the Bishops' Advisory group on Urban Priority Areas published *Staying in the City*. 'Urban deprivation,' the latter report states, 'is as bad if not worse than it was ten years ago. Many UPAs experienced considerable reductions in resources for mainstream programmes (especially housing).' Sadly, however, it seems that most people are anaesthetised by research and statistics.

In recent years, many responses to homelessness have been promoted in London, resulting in dramatically reduced levels of homelessness. Some initiatives have extended to the provinces but, as an MP once told Trevor, sensitivity is greater in the capital because that is where MPs live and work and where they are most aware of the problem.

It remains an offence in England and Wales to sleep on the streets. Yet many people have no alternative. Without a home you have no address. Without an address it's hard to find work. Without work it's difficult to sustain accommodation. And without accommodation you're homeless.

Reasons for homelessness

There are as many reasons for homelessness as there are homeless people - and each one's experience is different. People tend to think of homelessness in terms of the problems it causes. A better approach is to understand the problems that give rise to it.

The principal reasons for homelessness include: loss of job; family and marital breakdown; the need to get away from a previous location/situation; lack of affordable housing; drug and alcohol addictions; effects of poverty, the recession or unemployment; discharge from prison, care or long-stay hospital.

Cultural and social change

We live in an age where, increasingly, people are living alone or in small households. This is a result of the breakdown of family life and cultural changes, including the fashion of living alone. These together with increased life expectancy mean that more people require more accommodation units than in any previous generation.

Marital breakdown is a major factor. Two or three generations ago mum and dad would live with their children and maybe even with their own parents in a single accommodation unit. Today the divorce rate is rising towards 1 in 2 and as families separate they need two units instead of one. If one of the divorced parties gets married again, given that the chances of further marital break-up are greater than in the first marriage, then the single unit required by the original set of relatives may have grown to three or four. In addition, young people leave home at an earlier age than previously, whether through choice or necessity. The same family then requires even more accommodation units.

Political policy

Jimmy spent thirty four years in a psychiatric hospital. Committed as a child because he was having difficulties learning at school and not, he believes, because of any mental health problem. With the closure of the hospital, Jimmy was found bedsit accommodation in the community. Suddenly, this man who had lived in an institution with no need to budget, cook, wash clothes, dust or vacuum was put into a situation where he had to do all that and more. Needless to say, within a few weeks, he had smashed up his room - the frustration of not being able to cope burst out.

Much good legislation has been introduced during the 1980s and 1990s. Sadly, though, it has often not been fully effective because of lack of resources or by being put together hastily or without adequate forethought.

Care in the Community makes provision for people to live within the community rather than be confined to an institution. But the effect of Care in the Community, placing vulnerable people in the outside world, has left a shortage of accommodation. It has had effects both upon the availability of housing stock and on the way in which people on the margins have received care. For example, as Trevor observes from the people he meets through the Palace Gate Project, long-stay psychiatric hospitals have been closed before appropriate alternatives were available in the community. In our towns and cities there are now disturbed people on the streets who are either sleeping rough or in inappropriate accommodation and who would not have been in this situation ten years ago.

The prolonged recession has also played its part. Most of us have had to tighten our belts, but an increasing number of people in our communities are finding it almost impossible to live in a way which is appropriate for a nation such as ours.

Housing policy

During the last decade, housing policy encouraged the "right to buy", whereby local authorities were required to sell their housing stock. It seems right that people should be able to purchase the house in which they live and where the family has grown up. But, as Trevor observes, the housing stock has not been replaced to give the next generation the same opportunity. Indeed, the money raised by this massive sell-off is still in the main held within local authority bank accounts as, apparently, they are unable to use it to build new homes. A recent study commissioned by the National Federation of Housing Associations indicated that 124,000 additional homes would need to be found in the social rented sector each year for the next ten years. The actual planned output for 1994/97 is 53,000.

Increased legislation has meant that local authorities who were formerly housing providers have become enablers. This means that they now work to negotiate partnership deals and to determine need so that housing can be provided through housing associations and other private sector routes.

House purchase itself was presented during the 1980s as the best, if not the only, way to go. The benefits were clearly set out but not the risks. The UK is faced with a situation where many thousands are trapped in negative equity: where their house is worth less than their mortgage. Repossession results in homelessness and there is some evidence to suggest that when the recession is finally over and the housing market improves then repossession figures will increase because building societies will find it more advantageous to repossess than they do in today's depressed market.

It is a credit to Exeter City Council that they have stopped using bed and breakfast accommodation for families on the council waiting list. However, at any given time there are a number of families who for various reasons do not qualify for the waiting list and these are placed in a B&B. Reasons for not qualifying for the list include not having resided in Exeter for six months and being "intentionally homeless". (This latter category includes people whose homes have been repossessed or who have been unable to keep up mortgage payments.)

Where's the logic?

In recent years, government policy has supported families and individuals moving into bed and breakfast accommodation at least as a temporary measure. "Temporary" could mean up to a year or two, but it is questionable as to whether this system is an appropriate and economical way to house people. The cost to the government of an individual living in bed and breakfast accommodation is £60+ a week and for a family £120+. In some cases, this works out at £500 a month for a family, which, in Exeter, is perhaps rather more than the average mortgage payment on a three-bedroomed semi-detached house. The Housing Benefit paid to support a family in a B&B is more or less equivalent to the cost of a three-bedroomed house. Whilst the implied solution from that comparison may seem simplistic, acknowledging the political, social and economic realities, it still raises the question of whether tax-payers money is being used in the most appropriate and efficient way. Although B&B is currently used less by local authorities, proposed new housing legislation anticipated for 1996 includes the removal of the statutory requirement to provide housing for families.

Government policy has been based on a premise that 16 and 17 year-olds should live at home. In an ideal world this would be an important way of valuing and supporting family life. Sadly, there are many young people for whom this is not a realistic option. 16 and 17 year-olds cannot claim state benefits except in a few exceptional cases. Yet for many, staying at home is not possible because relationships with their family may have broken down irretrievably. These young people, already vulnerable because of their age, are thus placed at enormous risk because they cannot claim state benefits.

Jane was 16 when she came to see Trevor. Daniel, who was in his thirties, came with her. Jane was unable to claim benefits and had formed a relationship with Daniel, who could. So, they were living together on the streets, with the help of his £37 per week Income Support. Daniel was not Jane's favourite person, but rather than live alone on the streets with no money she was putting up with him and the demands he made upon her and her body in order to survive, eat and be comparatively safe.

The Palace Gate Project has tried to help many young people like Jane who have been forced to live on the street. They are excluded not only from claiming benefit but also from securing medium- or long-term accommodation, being unable to sign tenancy agreements and enter into other property-related obligations. Recent new legislation is making this already dangerous situation worse.

What is homelessness?

It is generally agreed that the definition of homelessness includes not only people who are roofless but also those living in accommodation which is temporary, inappropriate or unsafe.

On the surface, Exeter appears to be an affluent, middle-class, cathedral and university city. This image has been promoted for a long time, but the problems of poverty and homelessness have been increasing. Even now it is a city where it is possible not to see high degrees of deprivation unless you look for them: but it is a place where they are there all the same. Exeter's homeless people are found in a wide variety of places: on the streets and roofless; in squats, B&B and hostels; in bedsit and other inappropriate accommodation, plus a transient population passing through.

Roofless

On average, Exeter's roofless population, people sleeping rough, numbers at least fifty to seventy throughout the year. This is seasonally affected and falls to approximately fifteen to twenty in the winter. Although this number may sound manageable, proportionally it is higher than in London.

Over the past four years, the average age of people who are roofless has come down with more young people (ie under 21) becoming homeless. Most are men but on occasion there are women too. Their ingenuity in discovering places to sleep means that it is very difficult to find them at night. They need to be ingenious: many homeless people have woken to find themselves being beaten up by people coming out of pubs and clubs late at night and by others who pick on the vulnerable.

Squats

At any one time there are about thirty people squatting around Exeter. Squatting is becoming more difficult as the new Criminal Justice Act makes it possible to evict such people more quickly than before. Although the Palace Gate Project does not condone squatting, it does recognise that when, as during a recession, many business premises are boarded up it is no wonder that homeless people move into the buildings. Additionally, there are also people living in vans and tents squatting on other people's land.

But it is important to have no illusions about squats. The buildings have no running water or other services. They are often damp and unhealthy. Many people who live in squats suffer from asthma or chest infections or other health problems.

Bed and breakfast

Hundreds of people are living in B&B accommodation. Often asked to leave the premises between 9am and 6pm, they may be barred from the kitchen except for receiving the breakfast that is part of the package. So it is almost impossible for them to have other cooked meals. There are also inherent problems of multiple occupancy: shared toilet and bathroom, walls made of thin panel construction and lack of privacy - the total stress is considerable.

Friends' floors

There are at any one time up to one hundred young people in Exeter sleeping on friends' floors. They have left home either voluntarily or at the request of their families. Common reasons for this include friction with a new partner of either parent or the fact that the family is very poor and Child Benefit has ceased on the young person's 16th birthday. Such young people may try living with the families of friends, but such arrangements are usually short-term and they find themselves moving from pillar to post.

Hostels

Exeter has several hundred people living in hostel accommodation. These range from a direct-access, male-only hostel to hostels for ex-offenders, people with mental health problems and those having alcohol or drug addictions. There is no direct-access hostel for women in Exeter and this has presented difficulties for agencies working with homeless people. Few women are sleeping on the streets, but this is another example of the way in which problems are hidden in cities like Exeter. If such a hostel were established it would soon fill up with women who at present are tolerating dangerous and vulnerable situations rather than sleep on the streets.

Bedsits

By comparison with other cities, only a very small proportion of Exeter's total housing is used for bedsits and similar private rented accommodation. This is exacerbated by the fact that as a university city, there is a significant extra demand for affordable bedsit accommodation. In fact, university students occupy about 1,200 bedsits in the community. This absorbs most of what is available and the remainder is thus at a premium, enabling owners (for example, landlords) to set their own conditions, such as "No dogs", "No children" or "No DSS". Such owners are also able to ask whatever they want as a deposit or rent in advance. In consequence, most bedsit accommodation is unavailable to people who are in extreme poverty or experiencing differing degrees of homelessness.

Housing association and local authority accommodation

People in these forms of accommodation have long-term tenancy agreements, so technically are not homeless. However, it is the experience of the Palace Gate Project and other agencies that if appropriate support and care are not available, many risk a speedy return to homelessness. They are often forced to choose between buying food or paying the rent, electricity or Council Tax. All those payments are essential of course, but too many people are getting into debt and slipping through the net by losing tenancies and becoming homeless again.

Who is doing what?

Over the years a number of agencies have become involved in working with different groups of homeless people in Exeter. Increasingly, these organisations have realised the importance of co-operating with each other in order to provide a better service and to avoid duplication.

The Homeless Action Group provides information and advice, mainly for young people. The St Petrock's Day Centre is for all homeless people, particularly those in crisis need. The Shilhay Community operates a thirty-place direct-access hostel where any man arriving in town can get a bed, if one is available. The Lighthouse Centre is open much of the week, providing meals and activities for vulnerable people, including those who are homeless. The Grapevine Family Centre provides supportive accommodation for lone parents and pregnant women. Crossline run a soup kitchen one evening each week and also provide an important and useful counselling service. The Exeter Homes Committee, developed through the churches, provides a guarantee of the deposit that is so often the barrier preventing homeless people from gaining rented accommodation.

Getting a full picture is rather like completing a jigsaw and we should mention also the work done by statutory agencies through Devon County Council Social Services and the Royal Devon and Exeter NHS Healthcare Trust's mental health services. There are also voluntary agencies operating, including the Exeter Drugs Project, Insight Alcohol Services, MIND in Exeter and others. Each of these organisations needs the others and indicates how a comprehensive service is being provided; although within the jigsaw there are still missing pieces: the picture is not yet complete.

CHAPTER FOUR

HANDS ON, HANDS TOGETHER

George is a middle-aged ex-army officer whose marriage breakdown left him with very little except a drink problem. He was homeless, so finding him bed and breakfast accommodation seemed like a great achievement. But from that point on he deteriorated. It seemed as if the struggle to survive on the streets had kept him going but coping with a more settled lifestyle was too much. His friends know where to find him - at the rear of a shop in Exeter. Being available to offer care and support and a cup of coffee may be more useful than trying to help people change into something they are not ready to become.

For many Christians in Exeter during the 1980s, South Street Baptist Church was a beacon shining with the light of Christ. For others it was a sign to be spoken against. Surely, the objectors insisted, the church's chief functions must be worship and evangelism? Wasn't the Palace Gate Centre just another specimen of that evangelical bugbear, "the social gospel"? Some of the members of South Street Church felt lonely at times as the criticism wafted towards them but they persevered with the work. The minister, John Stroud, is an evangelical at heart. 'Yet,' he once commented, 'saying this kind of work isn't central to the gospel has given me the most pain.'

Evangelical attitudes may have changed since the 1980s. In the words of one South American evangelical, 'To ask whether social action is more or less important than evangelism makes just about as much sense as discussing whether a plane depends more on its port or starboard wing!' Yet even if one recognises this to be true, the sort of work carried out by the Palace Gate Project might still appear unprofitable if subjected to a realistic cost-benefit analysis.

Much of the Project's work is unpredictable. An outstanding and encouraging example of this is Simon. For several months he dropped in occasionally at Palace Gate. One day he turned up needing help and admitted that he had been taking food and vouchers in order to save money to buy drugs. Now something (perhaps it was the care he had received) had brought him to the point where he realised the need to turn his life around. Aged 27, Simon had been taking drugs for twelve years. A violent man with a record of serious crime, he was now a quivering wreck, desperate for the help he had failed to find in any of his regular haunts.

He spent most of the next couple of months in Trevor's office, eight hours per day, going through a traumatic withdrawal process. Sometimes he was able to help with clerical tasks. He was afraid to go outside because he knew the dealers would be waiting to reclaim him.

A good deal else happened during these weeks. Simon had been given a Christian book by a friend who had been converted while in prison. Reading it convinced Simon that there was something which could replace the buzz which had hooked him on drugs. Trevor took him to see Tony who understood the problem. Tony told Simon that it wouldn't be easy to get rid of the effects of twelve years on drugs. Tony had a laid-back way of explaining his Christian faith and he also warned Simon that Christianity wouldn't alleviate all his difficulties - Christians had problems too.

Simon looked at the possibility of voluntary work with young people but realised he wasn't yet strong enough. He had been sleeping on a friend's floor but the landlord had asked him to leave. He was found good accommodation outside Exeter, away from the difficulties of his previous life and he managed to get work during the summer. One of the people he was working with was a professional diver and Simon decided he would like to become a diver. Since this would involve passing a medical test, he began running on the sea front and playing football. Somehow the money for the diving course came together and Simon earned his qualification.

'Reality is scary,' he said. 'I've never been here before as an adult; the last time I had clear thoughts was when I was 14 and every time reality came I took more drugs. I've always hidden from it and run from it and it's scary to be here and experience real feelings, real stress, real problems, real life.'

Simon became a Christian. He also became a whole person for the first time in his adult life.

If success means being married, with 2.4 children, living in a semi, with a car in the drive and a secure job, then more and more people are failing. But what if success is about moving one's life on and having hope for the future or about being homeless and unable to hold down a job and now living in accommodation and able to pay the bills? The Project's work is long-term, demanding, and the reason for doing it is not so much about seeing success as about being there, in a way that is constant and caring, that shows by its actions who we are and how much care there is for the people who go to it for help.

And yet, despite all that, despite all the support, all the advice, all the concern, there is still no guarantee of lasting success: a few months after the events described above, Simon committed suicide.

Was it worth the effort? Is the kind of work done by the Palace Gate Project anything more than a species of middle-class do-goodery? Or an emotional self-indulgence? Does it have any direct or close relationship to

Christian belief? Searching questions deserve serious answers.

We have already described how Brian Haymes raised similar questions in the 1970s and how John Stroud came to see a symbolic significance in the story of Bartimaeus. The work of the Palace Gate Project is not a matter of "mere theory" but has practical implications. It confronts those responsible for strategy and management by asking what are the objectives of such a project. If they fail to address these underlying issues they will not think consistently about priorities and will blunder from one *ad hoc* decision to another. If they are aiming at nothing they will surely hit their target.

The theological questions are equally important at the grassroots. The Project depends on the help of Christians from various traditions. Even within the same tradition there will be room for disagreement - not least, for example, about evangelism. Should helpers actively evangelise clients? Or should they be forbidden to speak about Jesus?

The whole question of theology is important and can be approached in a variety of ways.

Bottom-up theology

In a world top-heavy with bureaucrats, think-tanks, and over-promoted former practitioners, it is vital that the Project functions at ground level, working with people in need, in the crisis, in their brokenness: understanding how they feel and what they are facing. Bottom-up theology builds from being alongside people as distinct from sitting in the warm security of pew, study or committee room and imagining what other people may be experiencing.

For too long the Church *en masse* (all denominations, all traditions) has believed it knows what people should be given and has sought to provide this - but rarely asking whether this is what they actually *want*. A relationship of trust must be built before people are willing to share the deeper fears and concerns that underlie the more superficial needs they present at first.

Churches are middle-class and comfortable. 'History repeats itself. It has to. No one listens,' writes the poet Steve Turner. Over 200 years have passed since John Wesley left his ministry in the parish churches and university chapels of Oxford to preach wherever in the length and breadth of the country he could find an audience. The Methodist Church which he founded also became comfortable and respectable and less than one hundred years later, another Methodist, William Booth, found it necessary to leave Methodism and start the Salvation Army to be with people in need. Christian traditions in Britain generally follow the same pattern of lapse into middle-class comfort.

It needs to be recognised that when people become Christians, their lives are turned round, they are impelled towards new values, their standing in the community improves, they become more comfortable. But that is no reason not to give others the same opportunity to remake their lives. The church should always keep one foot in the gutter.

Social responsibility and justice

The Bible has a great deal to say about social responsibility and justice, siding with the poor and oppressed. So it's not surprising that so many churches of all denominations have social responsibility officers, justice and peace committees and so on. Much of what they do, however valuable it may be, is intended to support and encourage work of social responsibility that is being carried out elsewhere by other people. It is more difficult to support and be involved in such work in one's own city. Easier, perhaps, to pray for other countries and write to a government minister or MP about something that is happening 500 miles away, than to get involved in a local community project. But this is precisely what the Palace Gate Project is doing: pursuing justice issues with a bias to the poor, standing up for those experiencing poverty, walking with people who are rejected and marginalised, outcast from the communities where they live. Many factors combine to make this work demanding and costly. The problems are there under your nose and they won't go away. You've prayed about them but they continue. You've given people hours of your time but still they come back. Still they are making mistakes. Still they are in chaos. Still they make demands.

To the extent that church members realise this they may well feel relieved that their social responsibility is being shouldered by someone else, so that they are absolved of any responsibility. Of course we can't all be expected to feel the same involvement or concern about every issue. But in Exeter, the good news is that local churches have been very supportive. They are kept informed of all the ideas developed by the Project. Their response is seen in the way people volunteer to help and in financial support, some of which is regular and long-term, and by commitment to prayer.

Reconciliation

The Church should be in the business of reconciliation. But it would be easy for anybody looking at the different denominations to conclude that it is not a part of the Church's message and ministry. So it has come as a pleasant surprise that the Project has received practical help and volunteers from churches across the denominations. The way in which these people got on with the job, worked so well with each other and enjoyed friendship within their teams is good news. Christian unity is achieved more through shared action than through struggling with questions about theology and styles of worship. Once Christians have become friends in this way they will find it more difficult to fall out over the comparatively little they do not have in common.

Another form of reconciliation has been the way in which the Palace Gate Project has brought together agencies in the city. Contacts have been made both with other voluntary sector agencies and also with statutory agencies.

In all the Project's work and contact with others, no one player is in a position to provide every aspect of every service. Yet the work has been possible because people have worked together and trusted each other. The sum of the parts has been greater than the total of their isolated contributions. This is a good model for the Church as a whole and for the wider community: listening to one another, trusting one another and working together to build a better community.

Unconditional love

Trevor grew up in the church, trained as a local preacher and was familiar with the idea of unconditional love. But it was only when he became a Community Development Worker with the Palace Gate Project that he began to understand what it actually means.

Loving unconditionally is not something the age in which we live knows much about: we tend to want something in return for most of the things we do. It is not easy to love for love's sake: to care and go on caring, not for a response, not for a reaction, not to change people. It is difficult and demanding. Unconditional love requires constancy. It's not like a hobby, taken up as the autumn nights draw in and dropped before Christmas because it has become boring or difficult and the time has come to try something new. Caring for people, offering them unconditional love, means going on day after day. It means work that is tough, stressful, demanding.

Unconditional love means not working to our own agenda but "being there" and getting alongside people in their need and brokenness.

Shalom

Others associated with the Project understand the work in terms of the biblical concept of *shalom* or peace. Michael Selman, Rector of the Central Parish, found here an answer to the questions he was compelled to ask about the role of a city-centre church:

'If it sees itself merely as a cell of the Church of England, such a church may continue to function more or less as parish churches have done since time immemorial. Most people expect the parish church to concern itself with religious or "spiritual" matters within its own parish. However, if it seeks its mandate from the gospels it finds itself commanded to preach the Good News of the kingdom of God and to heal the sick. How that is understood may be open to question but it certainly involves a recognition of God's concern for all people in every aspect of life.

'For the Bible points to a God whose relationship with his world touches the whole of existence. Salvation is not a narrowly "religious" matter, but involves freedom from need and anxiety: a state which is described as *shalom*. The word is usually translated as "peace" but it is much more than the absence of war and conflict, though it certainly implies that blessing. Sometimes the word describes what we would call "health", often it entails harmony and balance. To be in *shalom*, at peace, is to be restored to our proper relationship with God, with others and with ourselves. It is more than an individual state, for it cannot be separated from our place in the community. Indeed, the Old Testament, in particular, hardly has a concept of individual peace or salvation.

It is the whole society which either is, or is not, in harmony with the Lord.

'The Good News of the gospel is that God's kingdom is breaking in to transform the world; and the Church is committed to proclaiming this emerging peace of Christ, not only with words but also with actions that promote *shalom*, and brings healing to individuals and to the nations. Forgiveness of sins is an essential part of this, but so is working for reconciliation and justice. The miracle of the gospel message is that God loves us, and calls us to share that love, and that peace which 'passes all understanding', with others.

'We cannot enjoy *shalom*, unless we want to see others enjoying it, and that draws the Church into ministering to others, perhaps especially those who are marginalised.'

Prayer: The Gatehouse Movement

Christians believe the power of prayer affects both individuals and organisations. Sometimes this may happen through direct divine intervention, sometimes because as people pray they come to perceive the world in a different way, recognising needs and realising that they themselves may become part of the solution to the problems they are praying about.

The Gatehouse Movement started in 1993. Trevor Gardner and Mary Cotes had been talking with Richard Frost and they felt the need for a directly spiritual approach to a number of issues. These included the work of the Project in general, the painful areas of peoples' lives that were being presented within this and also the bigger issues connected with homelessness, both locally and nationally.

The Gatehouse Movement was set up by Richard to enable people within the local Christian community to pray specifically for homelessness issues. It was all very well during Sunday services for congregations to "pray for the homeless" - but what was needed was *informed* prayer. Initially, the Gatehouse Movement, enabled this to be done in three specific ways.

Firstly, by setting up a telephone prayer line giving prayer concerns, updated every two weeks and available to any who wanted to pray for these issues.

Secondly, bi-monthly prayer groups were set up in homes in different areas of the city. These brought together Christians of all denominations praying for individuals requiring prayer, for the workers of the Palace Gate Project and other projects dealing with homelessness around the city and also for a vision of how this work could lead to a more appropriate way of helping homeless people in the future.

Thirdly, Gatehouse brought the individual prayer groups together twice a year for a united prayer meeting and has also helped to organise and promote a service on Homelessness Sunday, held every November.

After a year, the telephone prayer line was stopped since it was not used as much as was expected. It was replaced by providing a monthly prayer letter which is available to anyone willing to send stamped addressed envelopes to receive it. This has redirected resources and reduced costs. (In order to preserve confidentiality the names of individuals mentioned on the prayer sheet, as in this book, are changed - God knows how to identify the people being prayed for.)

What about answers to prayer? These have been seen by the remarkable way in which things have happened: so much achieved by the Project; the staff constantly refreshed, strengthened and enabled to continue; the completion of the St Petrock's Day Centre came to fruition with so few setbacks; and in the way that individual lives have been changed. On many occasions accommodation or practical needs have been met soon after they were mentioned to those who pray.

There is no doubt that these achievements are due to the way in which homeless individuals and the Palace Gate Project itself are supported by so many unknown, unnamed people whose contribution is to pray.

The Project and the kingdom of God

So, what is our response to the question, "Why should the Church care about homeless people?"?

As we have suggested, the concept of *shalom* and of God's unconditional love requires Christians to have a concern for social responsibility and justice for all. For Christ died for all, as part of his task of proclaiming and bringing the kingdom of God. This kingdom is not a place or an institution (neither is it the Church!). Rather it is the re-establishment of God's sovereign rule over his creation.

The coming of the kingdom involves dealing with the effect of sin and evil in peoples' lives. So Jesus pronounces forgiveness, but he also set people free from the power of evil and restores to others their sense of dignity and their place in the community which has been denied them because of their state. So lepers are cleansed and sinful people and outcasts are treated with courtesy and respect. In the life and ministry of Jesus we see the restoration of harmony and *shalom* which are central to the biblical understanding of salvation.

Sometimes in the gospel we see clear signs of conflict, between the values of "the world" and those of the kingdom. Christians are encouraged not to conform to this fallen world, but to be transformed by the experience of God's love and power:

> 'Therefore, I urge you...in view of God's mercy, to offer your bodies as living sacrifices, holy and pleasing to God - which is your spiritual worship. Do not conform any longer to the pattern of this world, but be transformed by the renewing of your mind.' (Romans 12:1-2.)

Our lifestyle is to be radically different from that of our frequently judgmental and grasping society. We are to be imitators of Christ, who emptied himself for the sake of others and gave his life in service to them.

The grace of God is offered to all unconditionally. Grace is God's free gift of himself to his world in love. This gift in turn enables us to respond to God in worship and praise and to other people in acceptance and love. We receive grace in order to give it away. Grace is not, and cannot be, earned. Thus it challenges a world which insists on benefits being restricted to those who have earned them. The good news is that God does not reject those who "fail". The only condemnation in the gospels is for those who do not acknowledge their need of grace.

The Palace Gate Project must be a service where all are valued, regardless of their standing in the world's eyes. It also challenges the world's favouritisms. In the kingdom, there is no distinction between deserving and undeserving poor. The value and dignity of all users is to be affirmed; a tendency to greet some and ignore others is unacceptable.

In the kingdom of God poverty is valued. This challenges the world's fears and anxieties about its own poverty - in terms of skills, finances, personnel and individuals who are materially poor.

The kingdom of God holds surprises. This challenges the closed minds of both world and Church. The Project must guard against attitudes which stereotype people and stunt creative growth. Openness is important if the kingdom is to break in and surprise us in ways we cannot yet imagine.

The work of the Project and all who are Christians is a high calling and a demanding task with tremendous rewards, reflecting that which Christ gained for all through his crucifixion and resurrection.

CHAPTER FIVE

THE VOUCHER SCHEME

The next few chapters provide information on the setting up and operation of the various services which have stemmed from the Palace Gate Project. The Voucher Scheme, which is described in this chapter, was one of the first and is certainly the simplest!

The Voucher Scheme is a straightforward, safe and efficient way of supplying food to homeless and hungry people. It was born from the need to provide food on days when it could not be obtained from soup kitchens or other facilities - a problem which is most acute at weekends. There was also a sense that people in Exeter were willing to help homeless people but reluctant to give money to beggars in the knowledge that it might not be spent in a way they would wish.

Towards the end of 1991, Trevor and a small team researched the possibility of a food voucher system and identified two small schemes in Bournemouth and Canterbury. Both were run by clergymen, who wrote vouchers more or less on the back of envelopes. It became clear that a strategy would have to be designed for Exeter. The scheme must be fraud-proof and it must be impossible to exchange vouchers for money, alcohol or tobacco. Vouchers must be exchangeable at food outlets throughout the city, offering a range of foods and values and opening at different times. Initially four outlets agreed to participate: a small cafe, a fast food restaurant, a sandwich bar, and the Coffee Shop run by South Street Baptist Church at the Palace Gate Centre.

The arrangements are simple. The vouchers are printed in two-colours and serial-numbered for reasons of security. They have a face value of £1 and bear details of the outlets where they can be exchanged. Having bought them, the purchasers (for example, members of the public, church leaders, agencies in the city) may choose to distribute them personally or else buy them for the Project to distribute.

The vouchers have a six-month expiry date. This is mainly for auditing purpose and works well, since most vouchers are presented within this time. Purchasers may return unused vouchers to the Project, which then reissues them with a new six-month expiry date.

On presenting the voucher(s) at the food outlet, the homeless person receives the food and drink requested - but no change. Once a month, the outlets where the vouchers are exchanged send them with an invoice to the Palace Gate Project, where they are redeemed and a cheque sent by return of post. No commissions are paid, there is no administration charge and the value of the transaction at the food outlet usually totals within a few pence of the voucher value.

Although it costs about £200 to print 4,000 vouchers, the scheme has broken even so far since a number of the vouchers sold to members of the public are not presented at food outlets. There are various reasons for this: the purchasers don't get round to giving them away, or they lose them, or the people they give them to discard the voucher. For every such voucher "lost" in these ways, the Palace Gate Project makes £1: so far, this has paid for printing costs.

The Voucher Scheme has proved to be very successful. It started in October 1992 and by December 1995, 8,600 £1 vouchers had been sold. Many enquiries about it have been received from other projects throughout the country. Although business pressures have forced a couple of food outlets to withdraw others have taken their place.

Over the years it has become clear that the most benefit is obtained from vouchers purchased for use directly by the Palace Gate Project or, more recently, the St Petrock's Day Centre. Members of the public are glad, of course, to feel that their impotence has been overcome and that they can offer practical help to people begging in the street but the Project workers are in a position to give vouchers not only to people in need but those whose need is greatest. Experience has shown that not all who beg in the streets are among the most needy, although they clearly have needs. In fact, it is even possible that the most needy are too proud to beg and do not stand out in a crowd. Unlike members of the public, workers at the Project and the Day Centre understand the needs and know where the vouchers can be best used.

CHAPTER SIX

THE SOUP KITCHEN & CHRISTMAS CARE

In October 1991, a month after he commenced working, Trevor produced a discussion paper dealing mainly with the problem of homelessness in winter. It included the suggestion that different church groups might nominate a regular evening when they would serve soup or coffee and rolls. The Salvation Army already provided a soup kitchen on Thursday nights and the Free Church of England ran one on Tuesdays.

A month later the Palace Gate Project management committee agreed that, subject to a decision by the South Street Baptist Church meeting, the vestibule of the church should be used. The estimated cost for the four month period was £1,000.

Two hundred volunteers came forward from churches and the wider community, eighty of whom were to constitute the core of the Soup Kitchen's work. Many of them had been aware to some degree of the need of homeless people but had felt powerless to offer realistic help, so were glad of the chance to do something practical. Other help was also offered: Shaul's Bakery pledged one hundred rolls per night and fillings were also donated. An anonymous donor made a gift of £1,000 and a separate bank account was opened.

John Burden, a retired building society manager and member of a local Anglican church, offered to be responsible for organisation of the soup kitchen. The volunteers had to be formed into teams and a roster drawn up, subject to the inevitable night by night emergency changes. Milk, bread, and vegetables had to be collected every day. In addition, there was a debriefing session after any kind of untoward incident. The consequences of slipshod administration could have been disastrous. Ultimately, John Burden was spending thirty hours a week in this work - a remarkable commitment, providing administrative help and practical care for both homeless people and volunteers.

On 11 December 1991, the first night, there were thirty clients. By early February 1992 the number had risen to fifty, mostly men, and sometimes up to eighty people. The police and the Department of Social Security had expressed approval and Social Services had begun referring people to it. The pool of volunteers had grown to 300 and the number in daily attendance also increased. Church co-operation was apparent in both prayer and financial support - £8,000 was received.

Although local church involvement was fundamental to the scheme there was to be no proselytising. This was generally understood by the volunteer helpers. On one occasion, however, Trevor found two enthusiastic young men in the toilet, supporting a drunken client and thrusting his head into a sink full of cold water - with the intention not of sobering but of baptising him! This was a one-off and the ritual was not repeated!

The whole operation was proving to be successful at every level. At this early stage of the Palace Gate Project, it was clear that the movement the Soup Kitchen had stirred had to be built upon and carried on in order that the momentum could continue and grow. The food and warmth were secondary considerations to the sense of community, friendship and trust that those who came were experiencing. The volunteers were overwhelmed by the way in which so many clients were prepared to open up to them and to share their problems.

Several clients moved from terribly inadequate accommodation and a couple sought employment in a way they would never have done so before. Through the Soup Kitchen, the Palace Gate Project was also able to help in other ways: working with other statutory and voluntary agencies, seeking advice and appointments with doctors, alcohol counsellors, drug counsellors and ministers.

Many volunteers gave help during the day in transporting and sorting clothes and blankets and in other tasks. In particular, Bill Bell worked more or less every day in the clothing store run at the Palace Gate Centre.

However, there were problems with the Soup Kitchen. The accommodation was now very crowded and it would be necessary to find more suitable premises. A few clients brought with them tensions, drunkenness and drug-related behaviour. There was an increase not only in the overall number of clients but also of "travellers" with dogs. The South Street vestibule, which was no bigger than a fair-sized room in a private house, had already become crowded, but now the atmosphere was volatile and on occasion even dangerous. The appearance of some of those who came with dogs was felt as a threat by others even if it was quite unrelated to any disruptive behaviour. Drug-dependency increased the likelihood of irrational behaviour and a substantial proportion of clients felt frightened and were themselves suggesting that the Soup Kitchen should close at this point. Questions had to be asked: Should the Soup Kitchen continue throughout the year or should it be shut down for the summer? What was the best way?

In March 1992 it was decided to reduce the provisions offered to tea and biscuits during the period from April to early July and to close from July to early September, when many of the clients would be moving around and the volunteers would need a break. It should reopen in September/October on a permanent basis with a paid member of staff.

This did not mean that homeless people would be totally deprived of support. Prominent among the helpers had been the Sisters from the Presentation of Mary Convent situated across the road from the Palace Gate Centre. Many of the volunteers, who had formed a relationship with the clients continued to help serving soup and sandwiches in the convent grounds. The blanket and clothes store continued to operate from the Palace Gate Centre.

In spite of this setback development work on the Soup Kitchen continued during the spring and summer of 1992. Fifty volunteers attended training sessions. The Nichols Centre (a training organisation for people with learning difficulties) offered to make sandwiches and rolls each day. Trevor contacted local property developers and the City Council in the hope of finding a suitable building for use as a soup kitchen during the winter of 1992/93. This last mentioned element proved problematic and at one time the Palace Gate Project management committee considered the possibility of using a caravan as a mobile soup kitchen, but this was not pursued.

In the event, there was no Soup Kitchen in the winter of 1992/93. Deciding to discontinue was a hard choice. On the one hand, the Soup Kitchen ensured that people were being fed. On the other, it was time-consuming, since, in addition to the hours when the Soup Kitchen was running, it involved a great deal of organisation, and generated heavy demands. The food was valued but the benefit was only temporary. It was true that providing the Soup Kitchen tended to reinforce and encourage dependence on charitable hand-outs, yet it was clear that for many of the clients the food was less important than the personal contact with the helpers.

It was acknowledged that the Soup Kitchen had put the whole Palace Gate Project on the map in a way that could never have been believed possible just a few months previously. The Project was being taken seriously and Trevor's opinion was being asked about homelessness and other poverty-related matters.

During the early days, John came to the Soup Kitchen several times, looking depressed and dishevelled. He had lost his job and accommodation and his marriage had broken down. When he remarked that he would be 40 years old in a fortnight's time, Trevor noted the date. But, two weeks later, when he remembered, he was running late. Trevor had put the children to bed and was due to open up the Soup Kitchen in five minutes. So he stopped at the nearest shop and bought a card from the limited selection. It was pink and tacky, but with the car stopped at traffic lights, Trevor wrote in it and addressed it. When John was given the card that evening he burst into tears. 'No one has cared this much for me for fifteen years,' he said. 'No one cares if I live or die. Nobody would miss me if I died. Nobody in years has remembered something I've said two weeks ago and then acted upon it two weeks later.'

The Project staff and volunteers realised then that they were dealing with people who were so empty, so lonely, so broken, that simple acts of care, practical demonstrations of thoughtfulness made a great impact in their lives. In view of this, it was decided to replace the Soup Kitchen by a daily drop-in service and to investigate the possibility of establishing a day centre. The decision was difficult but in the circumstances it made sense.

Christmas Care

Despite the decision to close the Soup Kitchen, special provisions were made for the Christmas and New Year season. Christmas Care began in 1992 and has run every year since. It has touched people's hearts and has been chosen as a mayoral charity.

'I'm looking forward to Christmas this year,' said Bob in December 1995. 'If it hadn't been for Christmas care last year, I would not be here now. I would have topped myself.' For many, Christmas is a time for family togetherness and much eating and drinking. But others, homeless, lonely, living in bed and breakfast accommodation or in bedsits, experience a very different reality. They may regard Christmas as the worst time of the year. Not only are they left out of the festivities, the contrast between their experience and that of others reinforces their feelings of inferiority and failure.

The object of Christmas Care is to provide a good quality service for two weeks using different agencies working concurrently but without overstretching any of them. It is an organisational nightmare but represents a remarkable achievement of co-operation among different organisations and agencies in the city. More than 100 volunteers offer their time and energy. Among them are some who don't usually look forward to Christmas themselves but who welcome the chance to be with other people and to bring happiness to folk who are worse off. Gifts often totalling more than £5,000 plus immense quantities of food, decorations and presents are donated. Christmas Care helps about 300 people each year, some of whom come every day, others just once or twice when they had no other means of support. In December 1995, sixty eight food hampers were sent to those unable to get to the centres providing Christmas Care. Alongside that provision, the five centres served nearly 1,200 meals. Among the donors who help each year to make Christmas not only bearable but even enjoyable are Marks and Spencer plc, who supply the greater part of the fresh and frozen food.

In one sense Christmas Care has been a catalyst, enabling city-wide action between groups who were already active in this way. At Christmas, it brings together five organisations - Crossline, the Lighthouse Centre, St Petrock's Day Centre, Springboard and the Spotted Dog Cafe - all of whom provide services throughout the year, in a co-ordinated way. Christmas Care caught the imagination of Exeter, and continues to run successfully.

CHAPTER SEVEN

THE DROP-IN SERVICE

Jill is a young woman with a drink problem who, when her mother died, left home in her late teens and began living dangerously on the streets. One day, concern and frustration led Trevor to lose his temper. He shouted at her: she walked out. But she was back the following day and as time went by Trevor recognised that Jill responded to his expressions of concern and disapproval about her lifestyle and at what she was turning into. One day Jill said, 'Nobody has shouted at me for years. You really care.' Her life is now less chaotic, she has found accommodation, sees her father once a month and has acknowledged her drink problem.

The experience gained at the Soup Kitchen shaped the way in which the Palace Gate Project developed. By identifying the needs of homeless people, the Soup Kitchen influenced the development of the Drop-In Service, the Counselling Service and, ultimately, the St Petrock's Day Centre.

The Drop-In Service proved to be the real hub of the Palace Gate Project for three years. In the main it provided a listening ear but also gave a very practical service. People of all ages came either for food, food vouchers, clothing or a bus ticket to get home. In many cases it was about finding accommodation and sometimes it was very difficult to work out why they had come except just for company and a cup of coffee.

From its early days in 1992, the Drop-in Service ran for three or four hours a day from Monday to Friday. For the first eighteen months Trevor worked on his own but by that time the work had become so stressful and demanding that, as he now acknowledges, he was almost collapsing under the weight of responsibility and the combination of physical and emotional stress. This was when Adrian Willcocks' and, later, David Denham's help was welcomed. Their involvement in the work of the Palace Gate Project as a whole was to be significant, as we will see later. One or two other volunteers also made significant contributions both in time and commitment.

Getting the job done

At first, the service was run from Trevor's office. In spite of a notice on the door showing the hours when he was available, people came every day at all times. This not only made his work more demanding, it was also very frustrating when it interfered with the administrative tasks which were necessary. Plans had to be worked out and influential people had to be contacted if schemes such as the Turntable Furniture Project and the St Petrock's Day Centre were to go forward. In the end Trevor had to harden his heart and make two changes. The first was to move his own office from the ground to the first floor and to be available for Drop-In work in the ground floor office only at the stated times. The second was, as mentioned earlier, to involve more people as part of the Drop-In team. This made it easier to pursue medium- and long-term goals alongside the more immediate needs.

Pressures and risks

During 1994, fifty people were coming each week for information, advice, a listening ear, and practical help. Some days a long queue would form outside the room, adding to the pressure upon those providing the service. To know that people are queuing outside one's door is stressful in any circumstances, but this queue contained people who were already angry with life, some having had too much to drink, some mentally ill, and all in a confined space within a building, the Palace Gate Centre, that was already stretched to capacity with other client groups. In addition, when someone came through the door there was no knowing whether they would need five minutes or an hour.

Trevor was amazed by how often people who didn't know him would spend half an hour first chatting, then opening up very deep issues in their lives, and then thank him, as they left, for all he had done. At first, he felt he had achieved nothing, but gradually learned, during the three years, how to listen in a way that he found demanding and tiring. But this was what was most needed and appreciated.

There was an obvious potential risk of violence. Jason was desperate, disturbed and an amphetamine addict. He was also dangerous, beating up his girlfriend was a daily occurrence. He needed £50 a day to finance his addiction and once held Adrian and Trevor hostage in the office for two hours, during which he hurled objects around the room. 'The fear of what he was going to do,' recalls Trevor, 'was worse than if he'd actually hit us.' Since the Drop-In Service started in 1992, Trevor has been seriously frightened on (only) three or four occasions, but one practical response was to ensure that there was always a "back up" person available. A panic alarm system was also fitted.

Other difficulties were experienced or feared when seeing some clients who were clearly mentally unbalanced and others who were 'high' or 'low' on drugs. While they form a minority of those with mental health difficulties or drug abuse problems, the unpredictability of their behaviour did cause concern on occasions.

There was also a risk to health. Some clients were carriers of lice and scabies or similar contagious diseases. One day when Trevor went to the doctor for a bad cough he was surprised to be sent for a chest X-ray. The doctor, who knew about the Project, explained that tuberculosis was on the increase and was returning as a health risk to and through homeless people. A report commissioned by the charity Crisis and published in 1995 also showed that tuberculosis was being diagnosed in 1 in 50 homeless people, and they were 200 times more likely to contract the disease than any other social group. The situation is worse now than it was thirty years ago and there is danger of a new epidemic.

Method and ethos

Too often, Trevor heard stories of how someone could visit government or council offices several times without seeing the same person twice. Interviews there were often conducted through a window. Furniture was screwed to the floor. Mistrust was in the air. From the start, the Drop-In Service was intended to be as informal and "unofficial" as possible. Confidentiality was total, although there were inevitably times when Trevor was given information he would rather not have known. Most of the conversations took place over a cup of coffee and in easy chairs. At first the only records were in Trevor's head.

But records were needed. As more people used the service it became more difficult to remember them all. As a team of volunteers became involved it was necessary to have some way of sharing information and of preventing one member being played off against another. In addition, statistical information was required in order to secure funding and to demonstrate levels of need.

A basic record form was completed showing a person's name, address and gender; housing status; length of stay in Exeter; how they knew about the Project; previous Drop-In visits and the reason for the current visit. Analysing these records for a ten-week period between April and June 1994 showed that

457 different individuals used the service. Of these, 187 were first-time visitors and 269 ongoing cases. 119 came simply to enquire about the Turntable Furniture Project and seek a referral form but others proved to have multiple needs requiring much time and attention.

The fact that the Drop-In Service, like other elements of the Palace Gate Project, was run by a Christian organisation could have given rise to false expectations. Some clients might expect a "soft" response, yielding to every demand. Others might anticipate attempts to proselytise them. It was important that the service, while being characterised by friendliness, care and helpfulness, should also be professional, balanced, fair and appropriate.

All those who provided the service were required to work to the same guidelines, showing no favouritism to some callers above others, whether because they were more appreciative or seemed in greater need. In addition, the service was not to be regarded as a means of continually bailing people out of their predicaments and thus taking away their responsibility to deal with problems themselves. Instead, the ethos of the service must be to increase dignity, self-esteem and confidence by standing alongside callers and helping them to see that they could take responsibility and deal with their situation themselves.

A good example of this approach was the way in which food and food vouchers were supplied. As soon as a new caller, possibly new to the city, arrived in the office, care was taken to ensure that they knew their way around the city so that they could sign on for state benefits, be enabled to receive the appropriate services and thus have an opportunity to sort things out. An informal contract would be agreed, making it clear that the Project would willingly sustain immediate physical needs such as food and clothing in the short term, and that food vouchers could be provided daily until the first benefit claim was received. This would be a maximum of fourteen days, usually less. It would be made clear that, while they would be welcome to use the service after this for help with budgeting and other appropriate matters, it would no longer be possible to supply food or vouchers as before. This showed people that they must be responsible for themselves after the initial period, unless some new crisis occurred. Generally speaking it worked well, and was respected by many callers who, like Trevor, didn't particularly like the "soup kitchen" model of supplying dependent homeless people with free handouts.

The Drop-in Service was developed and amended and fine-tuned and much of its ethos and procedure has been written into the practice of the St Petrock's Day Centre which now provides a similar service. A limited Drop-In Service is still provided at the Palace Gate Project's main office and this deals with people whose enquiries fall outside the realm of St Petrock's.

Things can change

The Drop-In Service never claimed to offer counselling but it highlighted the need for a counselling service. Trevor remembers listening to one caller who reached the point of being about to release a great deal of "baggage" involving experience of being abused as a child. Trevor knew he was not competent to handle this. They needed a more appropriate opportunity and a trained counsellor. In spite of the strain and stress, Trevor enjoys the Drop-In work: 'Homeless people are no different from anyone else,' he observes. 'There is a great deal to be learned from people who possess qualities such as honesty, vulnerability and openness - qualities so often lost in the rest of us or hidden by the masks we wear.'

John arrived with a mohican haircut, a dog as aggressive as its master, and a drug problem. He was bad news and the people he hung around with were bad news, and when they were on the drugs they were really bad news. But there was a dramatic change when John fell for, as he described, 'The most lovely young woman,' with two children. She fell for him too. Within weeks he was off the drugs, had changed his hair style, got a job to support the "family", and found a rented two-bedroomed house in the country. Love changes things - but it's not always this simple!

The Drop-in Service has never been advertised and most people who were asked why they had come said they had been recommended by a friend. It is encouraging to know that the service is appreciated - daunting also to think that for every satisfied customer today there might well be another tomorrow!

CHAPTER EIGHT

THE COUNSELLING SERVICE

Graham was 25 when he came to the Palace Gate Project. An intelligent and capable young man, in the previous week his employer had announced that the recession had hit his company and that since Graham had been the "last in" he would be "first out". Graham lost his job and with it a company car and mobile phone. He also lost a very attractive flat because the landlord was his former employer's brother and had been told that Graham would no longer be able to afford the rent. Now Graham was at Palace Gate begging for food. He was not, as people say, "too lazy to get off his butt". Yet within a few days he had lost his job, his income, status, transport and home.

The Drop-In Service offered people practical support, information and help that would enable them to lead less chaotic lives by helping to ensure that they had somewhere to live, regular meals and the income they were entitled to. With these in order, they should be able to address some of the more underlying reasons for homelessness. But there was also a need for professional counselling.

It was agreed that an objective of the Palace Gate Project should be to set up a counselling service run by Christians, rather than a Christian counselling service. To express the distinction in another way, the service must follow the clients' agenda rather than that of the counsellors.

However, the clients in the greatest need tended to be the least able to use such a service. This was for two reasons - turning up regularly at a stated time for a weekly session was too much for most of them, but also dealing with their problems in a systematic and structured way was too difficult for most who had chaotic and complex problems.

John Stroud was a trained counsellor and with Trevor identified four other trained counsellors from various churches who had offered their services. Sue Le Quesne, the new secretary at South Street Baptist Church was also a counsellor and had been involved in a counselling service in London.

Like so many aspects of the Palace Gate Project, the eventual Palace Gate Counselling Service (PGCS) differed somewhat from the original idea both in its aimed clientele and in the service it offered. It became obvious that the Project should not limit its concern to those who were officially homeless. To provide a professionally structured generic counselling service would be an invaluable resource to have within the Palace Gate Centre. Many hundreds of people used the Centre on a regular basis. A large number needed the opportunity to access a counselling service and making this possible was one way to show them genuine care. It was also felt that if such a service was set up it should not be restricted to the use of the Palace Gate Project and the Palace Gate Centre clients.

Trevor and John agreed there was a need for a generic counselling service since many of the varied and numerous counselling services available in the city - as perhaps elsewhere - were of a more specific nature. For example, problems regarding relationships are handled by Relate. If people feel desperate or suicidal then the Samaritans offer appropriate immediate responses. If the problems are related to alcohol or drug addiction or with mental health problems then there are in Exeter voluntary and statutory agencies providing high quality services, support and counselling. This would also be the case with HIV and AIDS related problems, rape crisis, women's issues, bereavement and many other areas. However, very few offer a generic service enabling people to work through less specific or specialised concerns - such as loneliness, work dissatisfaction, lack of meaning in life, coping with personal crises or major change. It was with these and other areas in mind that a role for PGCS was planned.

A small committee was formed to deal with administration and a paid supervisor, Richard Skinner, was appointed to provide professional supervision for the counsellors. Initially, Sue Le Quesne undertook preliminary interviews with clients to determine whether the service would be able to offer them help and which counsellor would be most appropriate. It was significant and encouraging that all the counsellors involved in the scheme had come independently to Trevor over a period of months, offering their services. Indeed it was this, together with the need, that had initially raised the issue of whether PGCS would be a useful addition to what was already on offer.

However it seemed realistic to make only a modest start - although at the outset nobody realised how small the initial operation would be nor how long it would take to gain credibility and support for the service. During the first year, 1994, just three clients were seen. Some members of the counselling team began to wonder whether there really was a need and whether the investment of time and resources in this area was worthwhile. Trevor, John and others still believed the need was real, having heard from other parts of the country that counselling services need some time to take off. This is mainly a question of credibility but another reason is that many people have hang-ups about the word "counselling". 'Counselling is something that other people require,' 'Counselling is something that happens when you are in a real mess.'

Yet slowly the service began to take off and more regular clients began to come forward. From the start the intention was to aim at a "trickle" effect in advertising but during 1995, a more blanket coverage of the city was undertaken, publicising the service through the library, doctors' surgeries, the mental health services, the Samaritans and other agencies. Referrals started to come at the rate of approximately one or two per week. PGCS is now engaged in responding to these new levels of demand.

Confidentiality is naturally a high priority and an essential aspect of working to professional standards. PGCS works to the British Association for Counselling's Code of Ethics and Practice for Counsellors, provides a comfortable sound-proof room and a clear simple, confidential, record-keeping system. While it was always felt that the service should be available to all it was also recognised that some form of financial contribution could reinforce a client's commitment to the service and the help on offer. This is explained at the preliminary interview. Whether the client can afford 50p or £2 per session (or whatever else) the fee is determined and agreed. For many, private counselling elsewhere is out of the question because it costs somewhere in the region of £20 per hour. The amounts collected are small and PGCS is still subsidised by the Palace Gate Project. Although the counsellors are not paid, they gain invaluable experience and obtain free supervision. All the counsellors provide their services free of charge but expenses are offered for travel expenses and car parking costs.

Counselling is not for everyone, but many people can and are beginning to benefit from the service that is now provided at Palace Gate.

The Palace Gate Counselling Service, like all the projects that have emerged and developed out of the Palace Gate Project, is still managed by the Project management committee. It is, however, anticipated that as PGCS grows so it may become free-standing with its own management structure and allowed to have a life of its own. However this point has not yet been reached in this particular area of the Project's work.

CHAPTER NINE

THE TURNTABLE FURNITURE PROJECT

Joe and Viv find life difficult coping with four young children and preparing for a fifth one. The standard of furniture in their accommodation is appalling and falls well below what would be described as necessary and adequate for any family home.

For many of the people who sought help through the Palace Gate Project the most immediate need was a roof over their heads. But finding somewhere to live doesn't solve every problem. There is, for example, the question of furniture. State benefits do not extend to buying a cooker, bed or bedding, floor covering or chairs. 'No cooker? You can get hot food from a variety of take-aways - at a price. No bed? If you're really tired you'll manage to sleep on the floor.' Living like this is hard on adults. For families with young children it is devastating. The "fortunate" few may be given a loan from one source or another, to be repaid with difficulty over a period of months. The increased financial burden this entails means that accepting a loan is at best a doubtful proposition for somebody who is already living on the edge of a financial precipice. When you have limited finances, how do you replace the three piece suite which has fallen to pieces or get a new mattress for the bed which the children have soiled?

By December 1991, after he had been in post for three months, Trevor was already pointing out this need and six months later it was agreed that a furniture recycling project should be set up. Called the Turntable Furniture Project, it would provide a service whereby furniture of all types (for example, beds, wardrobes, chairs, sofas, tables, white goods etc) could be donated by individuals or organisations to be stored, mended and checked for safety as required and then given to people who needed it. Clients, those who needed furniture, should participate in it on a referral basis, which would minimise abuse. An additional safeguard would be the use of a form to be completed and signed by those donating furniture listing the items given for use by Turntable.

Among the practical issues to be resolved was the question of pricing. It seemed reasonable to make some charge, especially as some clients would have received a Community Care Grant to buy furniture. But would the Trading Standards Office view Turntable in a different light if a charge was made? Would the Project become liable to pay a business rate? One possibility considered was to supply furniture free of charge but to make a charge for delivery.

The preliminary planning also took account of the need to work with other agencies interested in collecting and supplying furniture. The Turntable Furniture Project had been formally set up as a subcommittee of the Palace Gate Project management committee and Margaret Midgley, a city councillor, agreed to chair it.

At the end of 1992 the Employment Service promised a grant of nearly £30,000 for the first year of the project. The Royal Devon and Exeter Healthcare NHS Trust had expressed its interest in sponsoring if Turntable in return would deal with children's safety equipment, such as fire guards and stair gates. Grants from Devon Care Trust, the Farringdon Trust and the Northcott Foundation were received and British Telecom gave a computer and £500 to buy software. Exeter City Council offered the use of an old goods shed but before long extra space was needed.

The introduction of stricter safety regulations governing the sale and resale of furniture has also presented difficulties. In principle these rules were welcome, since they were intended to reduce fire risk. But if they had been applied to agencies such as Turntable, which were giving furniture away rather than reselling it, then the result would have been to deprive needy people of furniture, which was in any case identical to that in most "ordinary" homes. In the event, it was decided to give away all furniture thus avoiding the problem that some could not be sold.

Today, there is a reception area for receiving goods, a workshop for testing and repairing, and a display area where clients can see the furniture available. They are referred to the Turntable Furniture Project by social services, health visitors, GPs, Citizens' Advice Bureaux and other groups. The Turntable van is out every day collecting and delivering furniture all over Exeter.

Turntable is valuable to others besides the clients who use it to furnish their homes. Thanks to the government's Community Action programme, it's provided occupation for up to eighteen volunteers at any one time. All are otherwise unemployed and they welcome the opportunity to do something useful in the community while at the same time learning skills and gaining experience which will appear on their CVs when applying for paid employment. However, finding suitable volunteers and winning funding for them is increasingly difficult. Indeed, it was announced in December 1995 that Community Action is to be phased out, thus the future of Turntable is uncertain.

Lewis Crowden has worked with Turntable from its commencement in March 1993. Having personal experience of redundancy and unemployment, he recognises the importance of having a reason to get up in the morning. As manager of Turntable, he believes that the role it provides for the volunteers is just as important as providing furniture for clients.

Turntable Furniture Project is also a recycling agency and much of what it puts into peoples' homes would otherwise be buried in land-fill sites. Turntable is now firmly included in the city of Exeter's overall recycling strategy.

By December 1995, Turntable had collected over 11,000 items from 4,500 homes throughout the city and supplied furniture to nearly 2,000 clients. This is a remarkable achievement in anybody's terms. There are just over 40,750 households in Exeter, and the fact that ten per cent have assisted the scheme shows an impressive degree of public awareness over a relatively short period of time.

During Councillor Margaret Midgley's term of office as Mayor of Exeter (1995/96), Turntable was chosen as the mayoral charity. As recycling becomes increasingly important, so Turntable has acquired increased status and become better known and used. At times it is difficult to keep pace with the demand and supply!

Clients range from lone parents, elderly people, families where the former "breadwinner" is unemployed right through to people moving back into the community from psychiatric hospitals, prison and drug and alcohol rehabilitation hostels.

The furniture donated must be of the kind of quality which is acceptable to all: a soiled mattress which is no good to the donator is no good to a Turntable client either. Those donating furniture should ask themselves if they would be happy to receive it. While not expecting shop-perfect goods and allowing for normal wear and tear, Turntable is not a dumping ground but a quality service.

As for Joe and Viv, Turntable stepped in and managed to provide all the basic necessities in order that their children and thus the whole family could receive better care and live in a place they could truly call home.

CHAPTER TEN

THE ST PETROCK'S DAY CENTRE

Once you begin to think about the subject, it's easy to sympathise with the plight of homeless people. Having no roof over one's head and being exposed to wind, rain and cold is an appalling prospect. But the hazards of homelessness are greater than we generally realise. For example, let us consider life expectancy. Nationally, the average age of death is 73 for men and 79 for women. Coroners' records show the average for homeless people is 47. People who are homeless are thirty-four times more likely to kill themselves, eight times more likely to die in an accident and three times more likely to die of pneumonia or hypothermia. As we have already mentioned, tuberculosis is now also causing growing concern.

Workers at the Palace Gate Project have become familiar with these dangers. Paul visited the Soup Kitchen twice. Aged 19, he was a drug addict with a common-law wife and a one week-old baby. One night he died on his way home from the Soup Kitchen. He had taken his normal dose of drugs but one problem with street drugs is that their strength and purity vary. On this occasion the supply was purer than usual, Paul had been ill, was undernourished and had been on other medication. Such a combination proved fatal.

Since September 1991, fifteen people known to the Project have died in their accommodation or on the street. All the deaths have been associated with drugs, homelessness or poverty and yet hardly ever have they been recorded as due to anything but suicide or an overdose. Nobody has made the connection. Nobody has asked the question: How many people die in this country each year because of despair, poverty, hopelessness, because of lack of love and the absence of accommodation? Perhaps it is better not to know.

Understanding the need

There's a general belief that what "the homeless really need" is first, food and second, shelter at night. As we have already seen, the Soup Kitchen did something to meet the first need. But it became increasingly obvious that material help was not enough. The full needs of the people visiting the Soup Kitchen were not being addressed in this fleeting relationship. As we have also observed, the need for the Drop-In Service became increasingly clear. To mention one typical problem - people were coming to the Drop-In Service with lice and scabies. A doctor might prescribe ointment or lotion but this was useless unless a bath or shower was available for cleansing before applying the medication and for washing it off later. Sadly, the city of Exeter had nowhere where a woman could shower and only one place for men. With unconscious irony, one leisure centre still displayed an ancient notice saying "City Baths", a reminder of earlier days when provision had been made for people living in homes without baths. "City Baths" had been scrapped when living standards had improved to the extent that almost every home possessed a bathroom.

There was a similar problem with laundry services. The obvious thing to do was to use a launderette. But launderettes were both too expensive and also embarrassing for people who possessed only one set of clothing. Nor was nutritious food available, except from Crossline and the Lighthouse Centre.

These needs had to be met in order to provide some concrete and continuing expression of the unconditional love on which the work of the Palace Gate Project was based.

In Autumn 1992, it became apparent that a day centre for homeless people was the long-term answer to the problems of operating the Soup Kitchen and to providing a more comprehensive service than the Drop-In. From that moment on, it was envisaged that this new Day Centre would provide practical, material, medical, emotional and spiritual help when this was required. A basic tenet of the Palace Gate Project was that whatever it supplied must be of the best possible quality, whether this was food, furniture, listening or caring. It was also important to learn as much as possible about good practice elsewhere and several visits were made to projects for homeless people in other parts of the country.

Finding a site

One of the six Central Parish churches was St Petrock's. The building could scarcely have been more central, being placed in the High Street near the junction with North Street, South Street and Fore Street.

In previous centuries it had been a prosperous city-centre church with rich endowments. There were now weekday prayers and occasional services but as the city-centre population had declined it had become something of a white elephant. Various possible uses had been explored but although the Parochial Church Council (PCC) felt a calling to help people in the heart of the city, it was not easy to see how best to utilise a church which needed repairs and had not been used for Sunday worship since 1978 (when South Street Baptist Church used it while their own building was being refurbished). When the Soup Kitchen closed, the PCC considered offering St Petrock's Church for this purpose, but the building was unsuitable, having no toilets, kitchen or running water.

The Cathedral authorities suggested that St Petrock's Church might be used for the Day Centre and offered the help of their architect. The PCC responded with enthusiasm. The Very Reverend Richard Eyre, then Dean of Exeter, convened a group to discuss the possibility of using St Petrock's. In November 1993, Michael Selman, as chair of the Palace Gate Project management committee, was appointed chair of the committee which supervised the detailed planning for the work. Subsequently, he became chair of the St Petrock's Day Centre management committee.

In financial terms alone, the task entailed raising £250,000. But the needs went beyond finance: it was not a question of merely appealing for funds but also sharing the vision so that supporters who had given money would be enthusiastic and still praying and paying for the project in five years' time. It was important too that the community as a whole should feel involved. The Day Centre must not be seen as the property of a small group, aiming to help a particular element within the city, but as a significant part of the life of the community. The intention, after all, was that local people who were damaged, sometimes violent and aggressive, should be helped to function better.

Problems

It was immensely encouraging to see this new project begun. But there were inevitably some negative feelings too. One reason for these misgivings was the cost and scope of the operation. Trevor was acutely aware of the responsibility he had for the way in which people were being drawn into a commitment which was far greater than anything seen so far and which might present unexpected hazards.

Once plans had been set out impatience was also a danger. Seeing fifty needy people every week at the Drop-In Service, it is immensely frustrating to think that this man or woman needing a bath today must wait two years for the accommodation to be completed.

At first, even the Palace Gate Project team were not one hundred per cent enthusiastic about using St Petrock's. If they decided to go through the complex process required to have the church formally declared redundant, they could expect a delay of at least three years. The alternative was to secure legal permission to vary the use of part of the church. Obtaining such a faculty from the Diocese of Exeter would be quicker, but it would mean that less space would be available for the Day Centre. The building's position was arguably rather too central. The ideal would have been purpose-built accommodation a couple of streets away from the High Street.

The person responsible for awarding the faculty was the Chancellor of the Diocese of Exeter, Sir David Calcutt. Before reaching a decision he had to consider any objections against using St Petrock's. The local Civic Society and the Victorian Society expressed concern about the scheme but didn't oppose it, asking only that it should be sensitively implemented. There was more opposition from some local businesses. To a certain extent this was based on prejudice, arising from stereotypical assumptions about "the homeless". But others based their objection on first-hand experience. Shops on Cathedral Green had had windows broken at night and suffered from the attentions of drunks during the day. Other people argued that providing a day centre would be counter-productive since it would attract homeless people to Exeter, not realising that all sorts of people inevitably gravitate to cities, including some who are homeless as well as tourists and business people. Others asked if it was really necessary to bring the problem right into the city centre. Might not a more suitable location be found three miles away on the Sowton trading estate? But homeless people were already in the city centre. Sowton was useless - homeless people don't have cars and can't afford taxis or even bus fares.

They need help, support and opportunities where they are, not where other people might like them to be. The Planning Department of Exeter City Council had their say and after discussion agreed with the proposed plans.

In his judgment, the Chancellor pointed out that the building had changed considerably over the centuries in response to changing conditions in the city. It was thus wholly appropriate to re-examine current needs and to use the building accordingly.

An architectural historian has described the interior of St Petrock's as, 'Among the most confusing of any church in the whole of England.' The chief cause of this confusion is the "new" chancel which was added in the 19th century and which, unconventionally, faces north. The original 14th century chancel faced east. A south aisle was added in 1413 and an outer south aisle in the early 16th century. The plan was to retain the earlier chancel as a church and reinstate it to its original glory. The Day Centre would take over the south aisles, leaving the 19th century chancel intact for use as a quiet room or for meetings. All the alterations would be internal: the original structure would be unaffected and, in particular, the view from the High Street would be unchanged. Entrance to the Day Centre would be on the south side, from Cathedral Yard. After several months, good homes were found for the organ and pews. The opening up of the interior brought an unexpected benefit:. It became possible to notice features that were unseen by most visitors previously.

Like most things in an imperfect world, St Petrock's is less than ideal and the accommodation is also rather limited. In the former nave there is room for a main seating area, kitchen, medical room and office. On the other hand, it doesn't feel overwhelmingly large and institutional. From the outset it was realised that the appearance of the Day Centre would say a great deal about how the people using it were perceived. The shoddy appearance of a cost-cutting environment would speak louder than word. So the specification for the alterations was deliberately set at a high level.

More planning!

In planning the Day Centre it was always felt important to provide the services that had been requested and needed throughout the time of running the Soup Kitchen and the Drop-In Service.

The primary needs were material and practical. The Day Centre was designed to have at its heart a cafeteria style room where hot, "home-cooking" style of meals would be available each lunchtime. Tea, coffee and other snacks would be served at all times that the Centre was open. The main room would also be an area where people could relax and talk with one another. Additional features catering for basic needs were a shower, bath, toilets, laundry facility and clothes store.

In addition, the emotional and health needs of homeless people needed to be considered. Because many homeless people have difficulty in accessing medical services, the Project negotiated with the Family Health Service Authority for the funding of a full-time post for nursing staff within the Day Centre to meet clients' primary health needs. Indeed, this may mean a reduction in NHS costs because until the Day Centre opened, homeless people tended to visit the Royal Devon & Exeter Hospital's Accident and Emergency department whenever they had any medical problem, whether this was a cough, sore feet or alcoholic poisoning. The new Day Centre was a more cost-efficient and appropriate way of meeting their needs. An important aspect of this medical care was also the provision of a separate room where people could come and talk with members of staff in private.

The response of the Exeter Health Authority (EHA) through its 'Health of the Nation' provision has proved to be particularly important and worthwhile. The EHA provided a lump sum to help towards capital costs and paid for the areas of the building that would provide a health benefit: the kitchen, the bathroom, laundry facilities and nurses' office. It is a great credit to the EHA that they have responded in new, creative and innovative ways. It was the EHA who felt that the Palace Gate Project, through the new Day Centre, could be best placed to reach the homeless people who were not accessing mainstream health services. The EHA were prepared to take risks and were the first to commit money to St Petrock's - this proved to be the catalyst that released other funding from statutory and charitable sources.

Adrian Willcocks & Dave Denham

It was around this time that Adrian Willcocks and David Denham come to the fore in our story. Both had been heavily involved in the Drop-In Service and had important roles in the planning of the Day Centre.

An engineering draughtsman by training, Adrian had a successful career in the building trade. He enjoyed his managerial role but wondered from time to time, as many people do, about finding a job which would be more fulfilling and of more tangible value to the community. But married to Tracy, he is a family man by temperament and conviction (and refused further promotion for this reason) and four young children were a powerful argument for staying put.

However, when asked by his employer to administer yet another phase of redundancies, he declined to do the task and took voluntary redundancy instead. The eldest child was 11, the youngest 4, but Adrian and Tracy decided he should take redundancy. It was time to reassess his life.

One important factor in considering a new career was Adrian's awareness of social needs. This consciousness had been growing since he had become Home Mission Secretary at St Thomas Methodist Church, where he and Trevor had been members for many years. Adrian felt the right course was to offer to work with Trevor for a year as a volunteer. This happened in November 1992, and throughout the following year, Adrian's managerial experience was invaluable. He was able to help with the development of the Voucher Scheme, Turntable Furniture Project and the Exeter Community Umbrella.

His gifts and experience were to be even more useful when the time came to plan the Day Centre. His building experience equipped him to assess the good and bad points of St Petrock's Church and to envisage what alteration and refurbishing would be needed. Adrian produced the drawings which showed the architects how the building might be utilised. In addition, Adrian's managerial and administrative experience enabled him to set out detailed guidelines and policies for the use of the different areas in the Centre, such as safety procedures and job descriptions - all essential if the Centre was to function efficiently and humanely. While it was being built, his site-management experience also proved invaluable. Adrian is also an effective fund-raiser and especially skilled at presenting the Day Centre to business people.

During 1993, Adrian worked more or less as a full-time volunteer within the Palace Gate Project, while continuing to enquire about jobs elsewhere in the caring professions. By November 1993, the Employment Service had agreed to pay the Project through their Programme Development Fund to employ Adrian as a Project Co-ordinator. Subsequently he was appointed as

Manager of the St Petrock's Day Centre. He reckons the job as a manager is not unlike his earlier one but it allows him to build on his concern for people. He believes it is important that agencies in the voluntary sector should make the transition from running on good ideas to functioning as social businesses in a professional manner.

One helper summed up how she perceived the differing strengths of Adrian and Trevor, 'I don't think the St Petrock's Centre would ever have got started without Trevor. And it would never have been completed without Adrian.'

Brought up in a Christian home, David Denham spent twenty of his working years in the motor trade. After leaving the world of automobiles, he sold building products for some time, before moving to an electrical wholesalers. This job ended in September 1993 after a period of illness.

Unemployed and having helped with the Soup Kitchen and Christmas Care, Dave sought out Trevor and offered to help in the office or wherever he could. He was receiving Sickness Benefit but the DSS were willing to accept his doctor's word that the work would be therapeutically helpful. Trevor asked him to help with the Drop-In Service and after spending some time observing, Dave decided that he might be able to help in this way too. Realising that he was being entrusted with an input into the lives of other people changed Dave's self-image.

From February to September 1993 he continued to work at the Palace Gate Project for two days a week, while applying for jobs elsewhere. As he saw more of the Project, Dave realised how much help Trevor and Adrian would need if the Day Centre was to become a reality. During the closing months of 1993 he helped to find equipment for the Day Centre and in other ways learned about it from the inside. He helped to remove pews and to dismantle the church's organ, which was sent to a church in the Netherlands. Although he had been warned that there could be no question of "jobs for the boys", he applied for the advertised post of Assistant Manager and he, like Adrian, was awarded the job on his own merits.

Funding partnership

St Petrock's Church came rent and rates free, there was no purchase price and there was a dowry that paid for external repairs. For a city centre site, this facility would ordinarily have been unthinkable. These facts also served to help other funding organisations to feel easier about entering into partnership.

Capital expenditure (building conversion and setting-up costs) and general operational expenses for the first fifteen months (staff salaries, electricity, telephones etc) required a total of £250,000.

Exeter Health Authority contributed £60,000. The Diocese of Exeter donated £20,000. Crisis have funded a member of staff for three years. other significant financial contributions came from the Church Urban Fund, Devon County Council Social Services, the Family Health Service Authority, Comic Relief, the Mayor's Christmas Appeal 1994, large national trust funds (who requested anonymity), the Palace Gate Project and local churches, schools and community organisations. All the money came in ahead of the opening date.

Many others, including the Employment Service and the Probation Service, gave valuable time, facilities and services in kind.

Room at the inn

Opening on Christmas Eve, 1994, as part of Christmas Care, the St Petrock's Day Centre officially opened fully on 4 January 1995. It started by opening Monday to Friday, from 11am to 3pm, as the Centre believes in providing quality rather than quantity.

The Day Centre commenced with full- and part-time members of staff: manager, assistant manager, secretary, chef and nursing staff. Due to an unexpected increased workload, a full-time paid supervisor was engaged in April 1995.

As the first year went on and with colder nights returning in the autumn, the Centre altered its hours to 9.30am to 2pm. This was a response to need: particularly for those who sleep rough and it has enabled them to gain access to a hot breakfast. As additional funding becomes available, it is hoped to extend to a seven-day opening with extended hours for specific groups and activities but this may prove to be more difficult than was first assumed.

The basic philosophy and purpose of the St Petrock's Day Centre is to provide care as well as practical and emotional services for people in great need and crisis. While it was always envisaged that these people would largely be those living on the streets, the wider definition of homelessness would include people in temporary and inappropriate accommodation. In the early days, the people attending included not only those in the worst situations, living on the street, in squats, tents, B&B and hostels, but also people in council accommodation or other more permanent forms of housing.

All those attending the Day Centre have emotional needs. Many feel they had no support mechanisms. Some had lost accommodation in the past or were at risk of losing it now because they had no one to talk to about debt or their disruptive neighbour or to gain help with filling in a form or in other very practical matters. Yet with some support they might maintain a good level of accommodation and avoid being drawn yet again into the cycle of homelessness.

St Petrock's Day Centre is about restoring dignity and pride in people who had lost those qualities and a lot more besides. This is one reason why the Centre makes a charge for meals and the shower and laundry facilities. The charges are very small and the services are heavily subsidised but the payment takes away the soup kitchen image of "us doing something for them". This results in more of an equal relationship in which, yes, the staff are able to offer help and support, but homeless people do not have to come asking for freebies. They can eat and wash and clean their clothes and receive far more with their head held high.

The benefit of having nurses - two part-timers who jobshare - on the premises has already proved its worth. The nurses' role has been central to the success of the Day Centre in enabling many people formerly unable to access medical services to do so. Only very recently a man came in to see the nursing staff with suspected tuberculosis. It was due to their primary health care that preventative action took place. This not only helped the man concerned but also stopped others being infected.

It is hoped that the Day Centre will never become a doss-house where people could just come in and vegetate and remain in their current state: but that it will provide the opportunity for people to move their lives on or to turn their lives around or at the very least provide a holding operation to ensure that people in great crisis and with very damaged lives would not get any worse. This has proved to be possible and is working - in many cases, people are either removing themselves from homelessness or having a higher standard of living within homelessness and certainly receiving better health care.

The workers at the Centre don't look for instant success. If someone has spent fifteen years in a mess, you do not click your fingers or give them a shower or a meal and think that everything is going to be okay. It takes time to build trust and effect change.

Costing in excess of £100,000 per year, the Day Centre now sees itself very much as a hub of a wheel with many spokes going out to the other specialist agencies around the city. These include the Probation Services, the Employment Service, the DSS, Social Services, the Housing Department, mental health services, hospitals, GPs, Citizens' Advice Bureaux, Homeless Action Group and many others.

When people find themselves homeless, then their first point of call in that need may well be the Day Centre where they can receive the immediate practical help and support that they require. However, the Day Centre does not pretend to provide a comprehensive service: it is really about partnership and valuing the expertise and experience of other professionals in the city. The role of the Day Centre is to provide initial support and help, offer options to people and to enable them to access services in other places which will be able to deal with specific areas of need in their lives.

Some of those who regularly visit the Day Centre have become vendors of *The Big Issue*, a magazine sold on the streets where a proportion of the cover price is retained by those who sell it (all of whom are homeless or have recently been so). Many of those who legitimately earn through selling this good quality national magazine have now been able to come off state benefits.

When Palace Gate Project staff visited similar projects before the St Petrock's Day Centre opened, they were warned to expect a "dead period" after opening. Several months might pass while prospective clients became aware of the new facility and sized it up, they were told. It didn't happen like that in Exeter! The previous work of the Palace Gate Project had built up trust through the Drop-In Service, thus ensuring that up to twenty people came to the new Centre from the first days. Throughout the first year, there has been an average of sixty people per day visiting the Day Centre, although on some occasions, up to one hundred attend: evidence of a degree of need undreamed of in 1991.

There has been no influx of homeless people from "all over the country" as was feared by some and if members of the public doubted whether such a facility was needed in Exeter, it took only a short time to demonstrate the urgency of the need and also show that the St Petrock's Day Centre was able to meet it.

CHAPTER ELEVEN

INFLUENCING THE INFLUENTIAL

It used to be, and perhaps still is the case that one never talked about religion and politics in the same breath. For some, there is a tension between political campaigning and Christianity: the former often aggressive and anti-government, the latter perceived as peaceful and subservient. Yet, the Christ who turned over the tables in the temple and spoke out against the Sadducees hardly matches the 'gentle Jesus, meek and mild' image of secular thought. Jesus never said, 'Be ye nice to one another.' Rather, his command to 'Love your neighbour as yourself,' (Matthew 22:39) leads to action which reflects a holistic concern for others: addressing both the strong and the weak, encouraging the good and challenging the bad. This love, this unconditional, perfect love, is one which also drives out fear (1 John 4:18). Thus, there are times when we have to address the sources of fear: the situations which cause people to be afraid - be they injustice, misrepresentation, prejudice, discrimination or the results of actions by state or individuals.

For the Palace Gate Project, Christianity and politics are interlinked and any serious analysis of the gospel sees that Jesus was also a political being. But what do we mean by politics? The Project has never been involved in party politics but recognises that most areas of life have a political aspect. The connections between every day life and our faith should be natural, as is the desire to improve the quality of that life for others. The Project is not afraid of getting involved in such politics. It is not afraid to stand up for the weak and speak out against injustice and oppression where it exists. It is important, however, that this is done in a balanced and measured way and not one which takes a particular party line and thus ostracises some of those the Project is trying to reach. It is the responsibility of all of us as citizens to be involved in our community and society and to exercise our right, responsibility and privilege to shape the world in which we live. It is all too easy to blame politicians. Rather it is important that we recognise our part within the community and are challenged to do what we can.

Representing the people

In practical terms, shortly after it commenced, the Project had soon recognised a need for a campaigning group which would address homelessness and housing issues. In 1992, a small group was gathered together and with Trevor arranged a public meeting at which Sheila McKechnie, then Director of Shelter, spoke. As a result of widespread advertising and media coverage, 300 people got off their settees in warm lounges and braved the elements of a wet October evening. The strength of feeling at the meeting was significant and subsequently a local Shelter group was set up. Sadly, due to changes in legislation, such local Shelter groups were dissuaded from continuing after 1993.

In December 1992, Trevor was part of a lobby of Parliament. This was organised by the Churches' National Housing Coalition and drew 3,000 people to London to meet MPs and present research carried out in every constituency. This research expressed housing needs and problems being experienced by an increasing number of people from a wide breadth of background.

The Project continues to see its role as including that of campaigning and lobbying. Letters are still sent on a regular basis by Trevor to MPs and decision makers. In the run up to the next General Election, the Project will again be exercising its role in voicing its view that those who are disadvantaged and, in many cases, unable to vote need representation.

Trevor has always felt a sense of responsibility in representing the churches in Exeter but he has the unique privilege in being an independent voice that has been able to speak out more freely than some others. Over the life of the Project this has meant that on many occasions Trevor has been approached by the media for his view and opinion regarding current news stories relating to housing and homelessness. This speaks volumes about the respect held by others for the Project and the way in which it can represent those with no voice of their own. The interest shown by the media has been overwhelming and has given Trevor an enormous opportunity to explain the needs, express the concern and articulate the response.

It is important not only to campaign and influence the media but also to speak to the statutory organisations and other decision makers. Much of the last few years has been spent doing just that. Many meetings and discussions have been held with city and county council personnel, employment, health and probation services staff together with voluntary sector organisations and business proprietors.

Trevor has also spoken to many churches, local community groups and schools. These have also been important areas of influence, where it has been a responsibility and a privilege to explain the work of the Project and those it seeks to help. Trevor spends a lot of time breaking down prejudices and stereotypes and explaining the needs of those experiencing poverty and homelessness. Trevor gives about two such talks each week. The impact of hearing about the reality of homelessness has disturbed the comfortable and well-off. Invariably, at the end of a talk, he is faced with a long queue of people - not just asking questions, but offering help and often coming with cheque book in hand (even though he makes no direct financial appeal within his talk). Many who hear express their impotence at not knowing how to respond. Trevor will also admit to not always knowing how to accommodate these offers of practical help: receiving them is very humbling but one also has to be realistic and not simply create work in order to satisfy kindness.

Changed attitudes

We now live in a city with a very different attitude towards homelessness and poverty. In 1990, before the Project commenced, such issues were "swept under the carpet" on the basis that if left alone, they would go away. There was also a large degree of ignorance about homelessness and its very existence in Exeter. This myth has been exposed and there are now many who recognise and understand the situation. In 1996, homelessness in Exeter is not significantly worse than in 1991, but the attitude, perception and understanding of the local community and its decision makers have changed considerably. Influencing others, as the Palace Gate Project and Trevor have done, is an important example that churches and individual Christians can and do follow.

CHAPTER TWELVE

THOUGHTS OF A "HOLY HELPER"

'On my first day as Community Development Worker I remember sitting in the office all day. It was a quiet day.

'On my way home, I passed ten newsagents and outside each one were the *Express & Echo* hoardings. Gradually, I began to wonder whether the words, "Priest Tackles City Drug Problems" might possibly have something to do with me (even though I'm not a priest). As I got nearer to home, I put on my sunglasses and hoped no-one was looking! I ran into the house and waited for our own copy of the paper to arrive.

'Sure enough, there it was: a front page story, with the headline, "Holy Helper Aids Addicts".

'I was appalled. How would this appear to the individuals and agencies who had been dealing with homelessness and drug addiction for so long, when the paper proclaimed that this new upstart had arrived and was going to take over?

'The Project management committee was angry and protested to the Editor. But after that there began a very good relationship with the paper. (Even though I did have to explain what the Project was *not* for several weeks afterwards.)

'All publicity is good publicity and looking back the incident is funny but at the time it was awful.'

In this chapter, Trevor describes how the practical experience of working for the Project has affected the way he understands his faith.

Acceptance

'I am often asked how many have become Christians through our work. I answer by explaining that one of the many ways we can help people is by talking with them about spiritual concerns, but because the spiritual dimension is one of many facets in life we are also equally concerned with physical and emotional matters. God has made us in his own image: body, mind and spirit. Until these three are acknowledged as of equal importance, we shall never be whole people. That said, it is not for us to force our agenda on people who come in a crisis situation: forcing them to speak about eternity when all they are concerned about is how to survive today.

'Although I rarely broach spiritual issues in conversation, they almost always raise themselves, often when people ask why the Project cares so much for them. Project staff have never been afraid to respond to such questions.

'If any of the churches supporting the Project at the outset perhaps hoped it would secure them a supply of pew-fodder then they will have been disappointed. The fact is that it is useless for churches to look to an agency such as the Palace Gate Project to provide new converts for them to nurture until the churches themselves are willing to welcome them. This will mean accepting people from an unchurched culture, people who don't know how to read and write, let alone when to stand and sit, people who will stick out because they are different in appearance and background and who will bring with them their hurts and their needs.

'Sadly, those we have been in touch with during these years and who have wished to fulfil the spiritual dimension in their lives have found it very difficult to immerse themselves in the worship and fellowship of a church and to gain acceptance.'

Learning from others

'It would be a great mistake to think that in an enterprise such as the Palace Gate Project all the "giving" comes from one side and all the "receiving" is on the other. I have learned much and often been humbled by the actions of homeless people and by their attitudes of humility and honesty and their sense of community. In particular, the "New Age" group that is often seen on Cathedral Green, with their drink, drugs and dogs on string, do have another side. Their sense of community, of fellowship and willingness to share with one another is unmatched by any church I have ever known. It may be true that they have less to give and therefore less to lose than many but, I have learned from and been challenged by those who are outside the traditional confines of the Church.'

Ownership and letting go

'At the Palace Gate Project we have come to realise that we do not need to own every individual service that springs from the original vision. Perhaps indeed the Church has too long been concerned with power, ownership and control. Contrary to what we often seem to believe, Christians and the Church have no monopoly on the best way of doing everything.

'It is important that the Project has worked with and on behalf of the churches in Exeter, responding to a kingdom vision, setting goals and responding to need, accepting risk and exercising faith. And who better to be involved in risky ventures than the Church that was set up to live and run by faith? I've increasingly come to see that the approach that has been used is the right one and a creative one that shares power and entrusts the work that has been started to the local community in order that local people can carry it on.'

Trevor believes in building for the kingdom of God, rather than creating a personal empire. He compares his role to that of a midwife: bringing to birth, nurturing, supporting and then letting go. He never wanted to be the manager of Turntable and decided not to apply for the similar post at the St Petrock's Day Centre. In spite of which and with the end of much of his hands-on work with homeless people through the Drop In Service, this has left a gap in his life and an experience of bereavement.

'I knew it would not be easy to let go of St Petrock's after working so closely with it, being involved in its conception and so intimately engaged with the clients it would serve. I found much comfort in what Group-Captain Leonard Cheshire said about the pain of handing over the running of the Cheshire Homes, which he had founded:

> 'We find it both difficult and painful to delegate day to day control of some activity for which we are responsible and which is of importance to us. If it is an undertaking that we have ourselves brought into being, whether in the field of business, social service, or whatever, it may prove almost impossible to force ourselves to hand over the reins because we tend to look upon our creation rather as we would upon our own child. We feel that a special relationship has been created, almost a mutual dependency which we have no right to disturb. Such was my experience. The act of delegating proved to be a thoroughly liberating experience.'

'I experienced the same fear and also the same positive outcome as I released St Petrock's to develop a life of its own.

'Inevitably, the years of work on the Project have shaped my thinking. Although it hasn't involved ordination, the Project is Christian ministry. It makes heavy demands. I'm not sure anyone can do community work at this intensity for very long, certainly not in one place. One person can only have so many ideas. The experience has prompted some hard questions about community work: How much is achievable? How many strands are sustainable, without entailing the failure of others? We're not doing anyone any favours by continually coming up with new ideas. When does the time come to consolidate what is there, rather than setting up something new? Will the time come for me to do myself out of a job and leave somebody else to run what has been established here?

'However, I'm convinced I could never go back to an "ordinary" job again! The creative demands and the independence have allowed me to grow and develop in a way I never could have done in the Inland Revenue!'

Faith and action

'Much of my work with the Project has been based on the words of the apostle James and in particular the second chapter of his letter.'

> 'Suppose a man comes into your meeting wearing a gold ring and fine clothes, and a poor man in shabby clothes also comes in. If you show special attention to the man wearing fine clothes and say, "Here's a good seat for you," but say to the poor man, "You stand there" or "Sit on the floor by my feet," have you not discriminated among yourselves and become judges with evil thoughts?'
> (James 2:2-4)

'These verses highlight the way in which it is so easy to treat people differently according to their outward appearance, dress or wealth. And yet there is no difference in the sight of God. Deep down, all men and women have the same basic needs, the same fears, the same hopes, the same humour and the same basic rights.'

> 'What good is it, my brothers, if a man claims to have faith but has no deeds? Can such faith save him? Suppose a brother or sister is without clothes and daily food. If one of you says to him, "Go, I wish you well: keep warm and well fed," but does nothing about his physical needs, what good is it? In the same way, faith by itself, if not accompanied by action, is dead.' (James 2:14-17)

'Saying, "Go, I wish you well: keep warm and well fed," to someone who is cold and hungry are nice words but it doesn't change their basic needs. The Project has been very clear on the fact that unless our actions equate with our words, then we are not true to the Bible and are not offering any hope or help to those we meet.

'Many times the Project has been offered substandard furniture or clothing. At the Soup Kitchen there was a temptation to provide processed foods. When St Petrock's opened, some felt the environment was too nice, that the specification we had used was too high. (One person told me that if we had made it a little more basic, then we would not have had to raise so much money!) Those who are poor, those who are disadvantaged, those who are marginalised, already have such messages reinforced to them time and time again wherever they go , by being treated as second-class citizens.

'We have proved that by offering people dignity and respect, by providing good quality food, furniture or services that this speaks much louder than any of our words and also confirms our intentions to care and affirms them as special and valuable people. And so as individuals, churches and communities we have been challenged by those in need to live out our faith by our actions.'

CHAPTER THIRTEEN

THE WAY AHEAD

In January 1995, South Street Baptist Church and both the Palace Gate Centre and Project lost two of their guiding lights. Having been at the forefront of the development of the Palace Gate Centre since 1977, the Reverend John Stroud moved to Suffolk to be chaplain to a hospice and minister at a Baptist church and the Reverend Mary Cotes, chaplain to the Centre for three years became minister of the Baptist church in Pontypridd.

John's role is described elsewhere in this book. His inspiration, wisdom and peaceful presence were greatly appreciated and admired by all who were connected with the Church, the Centre and the Project.

For Mary, the chaplaincy meant in effect being seen as the "official Christian" presence within the Centre. She was responsible for church activities in particular, but this did not include supplying an obligatory "Christian message" at each session. Nor was it about making converts. Being the chaplain meant building relationships with a great variety of folk using the Centre and being involved in all sorts of conversations from the most superficial to the most profound. Not surprisingly, Mary went to serve as minister in a church with a ministry among marginalised people.

Later in 1995, the Reverend Peter Webb took up post as the new minister of South Street Baptist Church.

In 1993, when John Stroud took a sabbatical, the Reverend Michael Selman became chair of the Palace Gate Project management committee. Michael has also had a very important and influential role within the life of the Project. In the early days this was perhaps in a back seat capacity as he was

Rector of the Central Parish and also had other responsibilities within the Diocese of Exeter.

Michael has remarkable gifts and knowledge and expertise in many fields, but is also prepared to get involved in the life of the city centre and to see the way in which this relates to the church.

Michael's vision and his faith in the Project and in Trevor are remarkable. He provides sensitive managerial support as well as spiritual guidance. For he, perhaps like everyone involved in the work of the Project, sees the building of the kingdom of God as being important and our role outside the direct confines of the Church as vital: to be involved in community, to be involved with those on the margins who are experiencing poverty, isolation and deprivation.

The initial application to the Church Urban Fund, made in 1991, had made the case for a Secretary/Receptionist. In the first two or three years or so, Trevor, with the able help of his wife Janet, fulfilled the secretarial aspects of the Project's work. At the beginning of the fourth year, a work placement was arranged with St Loye's College, a local training organisation, and Avril Fletcher came to the Project for three months. When the placement ended, Avril stayed on in a voluntarily capacity. At the beginning of the 1995/96 financial year, it was possible to re-work the budgets in order to finance the post of Secretary/Receptionist. On that basis, Avril was appointed for one year and it's been one of the best things that's ever happened!

For the first time in four years, Trevor has been "protected" from callers and released from many of the administrative duties - which has certainly made him more efficient! It has also meant that letters and reports can be produced accurately and quickly but the problem with having such support is that once you've got it, it's very difficult to manage without it. However, the funding for Avril's position is now hoped to be extended to March 1997.

Is that it?

Since 1991, the Palace Gate Project has achieved a great deal: including the St Petrock's Day Centre, the Voucher Scheme, the Turntable Furniture Project, the Exeter Community Umbrella, Christmas Care, the Drop-In and Counselling Services and the Gatehouse Movement. So, what remains to be done?

Even before St Petrock's opened, some of Exeter's other needs had become apparent. Here, as elsewhere, unemployment is a problem. A small working party began meeting in June 1994 to consider how help could best be offered. They soon realised that setting up a credit union could be a way of helping poorer people in the city to escape the clutches of loan sharks and the interest demands of banks. The working party took advice from people elsewhere who knew about credit unions and then, after convening a couple of public meetings, passed the scheme to other concerned individuals and agencies. Exeter City Council have seconded a part-time member of staff, via the Exeter Council for Voluntary Service, to help develop the idea.

Members of the working party have also visited other projects and attended the Churches National Conference on Unemployment in November 1994. Members have also promoted the annual Unemployment Sunday, held each February. But, unlike homelessness, unemployment does not capture the imagination of local churches and it is difficult to formulate tangible projects. However, the working party continues to meet in an effort to raise the profile of people who don't have paid employment.

Towards the end of 1994, both Trevor and the Palace Gate Project management committee felt a concern to know how the Project would continue following the establishment of the St Petrock's Day Centre. Homelessness was central to all that the Project had done and meant, both to the churches and to the wider community.

The first problem concerned identity. The Palace Gate Project was known throughout Exeter as being concerned about homeless people. Ceasing to work in this area might lead to a loss of identity. Although it would be wrong to take a hasty decision, a new focus was needed if the Project were to continue working with the backing of those who had supported it in the past.

It was also necessary to identify and prioritise community needs. The Project management committee met for a study day in February 1995 to survey the Project's achievements and to chart the way ahead. The intention was to identify areas of need in the city and marry these with the expertise and resources available to the Project. However, discussion showed the time was not ripe to take a firm decision about the future: there were so many areas of concern, so many groups of people marginalised, isolated or excluded for a variety of reasons.

Mark and Tracy have three children under 6 years old. Some would say they're fortunate in having a place in a B&B: warmth, a roof over their heads, food and drink. Some would think that - but only until they hear that Mark, Tracy and their children live in one twin-bedded room. Mark sleeps with one child, Tracy with the other two. Perfectly legal, totally unacceptable.

One significant and challenging development at the St Petrock's Day Centre has been the arrival of whole families. Among the one hundred people who turned up on one unforgettable day were no fewer than twenty children, with their parents. Being mainly in bed and breakfast accommodation, to them St Petrock's seemed an ideal haven to escape the barrenness of 9am to 6pm on the streets. But others attending the Day Centre needed individual attention, which was impossible to give in an overcrowded building. The last thing wanted by those who had come because they needed "space" was twenty children running around. Others, who were emotionally unstable, couldn't trust themselves near noisy and excitable kids.

It was agreed that Trevor should undertake some provisional research into their needs and should meet with the families to determine what other services and facilities were available in the city for them. If such were not available then it would be necessary to map out a possible way forward. There seems to be the need and also the will to provide a response: only time will tell this part of the story.

So, what happens next?

Another possible reason for apprehension is the question of how long the Palace Gate Project can go on working in its present form and with its current methodology. The problem is that the resources available in Exeter are finite. If they have to be divided among too many causes then it might prove impossible to finance a new development without terminating an existing project.

One thing is certain, this issue needs to be considered before March 1997, when the Project's current funding will end.

As stated earlier, the majority of the Project's money has come from two national sources, CUF and MAPP. In addition to this, many local churches from all denominations support the Project with regular or one-off donations. The income required to run the Palace Gate Project alone (that doesn't include Turnable Furniture Project and St Petrock's Day Centre) is £30,000 per year:

there has never been more than 20% of this funded locally.

One possibility is to consider whether statutory funding would be available. The Project is highly regarded by statutory authorities, but great consideration would have to be given before application was made. One of the advantages of the Project is its freedom to work in areas where it sees gaps in other services and also in campaigning and publicising injustice. This would be more difficult if statutory funding was received. There is also a certain amount of "dependence" that is created: in other words, because government departments often award tenders and contracts on an annual basis, any loss of such arrangements would result in immediate withdrawal of funding.

The future of the Project might be addressed and perhaps solved if the churches of Exeter and beyond agreed on the need to maintain a community project in the same form or whether a different model could be explored and commit the funding for it. For instance, a community worker might be offered for attachment to a local congregation for a three-month period, to help plan, resource and bring into being pieces of community work that the church might lack the experience or expertise to tackle unaided. This very different, though equally valid, model would require the commitment of many local churches both to recognise the need and also to support it with long-term, local finance. Certainly this will have to be done somehow from 1997, since no further pump-priming or other funding will be available nationally from church-based organisations.

At present, the Project's medium-term continuance is assured and its provisional agenda is set. The longer term is not so certain and Trevor is not convinced that there will be a need for the Palace Gate Project to become so established that it has to carry on for the sake of it. However, he does recognise that the name, reputation and track record of the Project has taken time and effort to establish. The hard work is done and it would be wrong to finish without thinking long and hard about it.

If, after reading this book, you would like to contribute towards the ongoing and future work of the Palace Gate Project, then please contact the Project at the address shown in Appendix 4.

Another important consideration connected to the future of the Project, which may even prove to be the deciding factor, is the future political situation. As things are, the purchaser/provider contract culture encourages the churches and other caring organisations to become directly involved in creatively responding to the increasing community needs for welfare and support.

These are exciting times, not least for those in Exeter who have seen churches being true to the gospel and responding to current needs. The Project has challenged churches to be seen by the wider community as relevant, alive and professional in their response to ever-changing needs.

Breaking the chain

Nick has been known to the Project since the very beginning. A well-respected member of the homeless community, he was often under enormous pressure because of the demands put on him by other homeless people who shared their problems with him. Nick is an alcoholic and never came to Trevor to seek help: only a listening ear. He comes from London, where he has a very supportive family. He has a trade and has often been employed. But Nick has always been attracted back to Exeter and to unemployment, alcohol and homelessness. Trevor spent many hours wondering how this cycle could be broken. One evening, Nick was returning home to his place in the park.

Drunk, he jumped over a fence and fell fifteen feet where he remained on the ground all night. He was found the next morning. Nick could have died but was taken to hospital with complicated fractures and a crushed spine. He was transferred to London to be near his family. Although told he would probably never walk again, due to the commitment of the medical team and Nick's own perseverance and determination, he now walks with crutches. Still living in London, Nick also has permanent accommodation and appropriate support, advice and practical help. It's sad that it took a major, life-threatening event, as Nick said, 'To bring me to my senses.' Nick keeps in touch with Trevor and says he'll visit his old Exeter haunts and friends again. We hope he will: but we also hope he'll go home again and not get involved once more in the downward spiral. Nick appreciates all that's been done and all that he's done to break the chain of poverty, drink and homelessness to put his family and own security first.

The story of the Palace Gate Project cannot be told in full. Partly because it has included so many characters and partly because we have not yet come to "The End". One reason for telling it now is the expectation that more and more people in Exeter, as they read it, will want to help write the next chapter. Another is the hope that readers in other towns and cities may find themselves thinking, 'We could do that!' - and begin their own story.

APPENDICES

APPENDIX ONE: AIMS OF THE PALACE GATE PROJECT

1. To engage in and support community development work in the centre of Exeter.

2. To be open to areas of unmet need and possibility, among both residents and visitors.

3. To co-operate with the Palace Gate Centre, other community centres and voluntary groups, to explore with them new possibilities, and to provide support and encouragement.

4. To encourage churches in the city to develop an appropriate Christian response and to work together in community-based outreach, developing closer links between churches and other voluntary and statutory groups.

5. To initiate new, appropriate projects and enable them to become autonomous wherever possible, with particular respect to (i) unemployed people; (ii) people with mental health difficulties; (iii) people with learning difficulties and other disabilities; (iv) lone parents and families in inadequate housing; (v) other homeless people.

6. To support individuals who are marginalised and powerless, through advocacy and appropriate action.

7. To show Christian involvement in community concerns through the development of networks and consultancy.

APPENDIX TWO: THE ST PETROCK'S JUDGMENT

After describing the changes proposed, Sir David Calcutt, acting in his capacity as Chancellor of the Diocese of Exeter, observed that the various formal objections received came from only a few people. He pointed out that it had been 'sensibly agreed between the parties' that he should settle the matter 'simply on written representation'.

Paragraphs (1) to (3) of the Judgment state that it followed an inquiry by Sir David Calcutt into a petition, made on 28 May 1993, for permission (a "Faculty") to re-order St Petrock's Church.

4. The Church of St Petrock is in many ways a highly unusual church. It occupies a significant position in the ancient city centre. The chequered history of the Church is briefly but helpfully set out in a pamphlet entitled *Exeter: St Petrock's*. It is significant, in my view, that the building has been adapted, from time to time, to meet the changing needs of each generation.

5. The petitioners' proposals have, not surprisingly, attracted a good deal of interest: there has been disapproval of what has been proposed as well as support. Opponents of the proposals include traders and other people working in the immediate vicinity of the Church; and I have seen the "Petition" which was apparently received in the Registry at the beginning of March 1994. Those who support the petition include the Diocesan Advisory Committee, the Dean and Chapter (and the Dean in his personal capacity), the Council for the Care of Churches, English Heritage, and the Exeter Health Authority.

6. The physical features are illustrated in a series of architectural drawings which have been considered and approved by the Diocesan Advisory Committee, and which are now available to me. There are two features to

which I would particularly draw attention. First, it appears that parts of the building will be retained for worship, and that they will be separate from the proposed Day Centre. Secondly, although there will plainly be some structural changes, those changes will not be of such a kind that, if a future generation should wish it, the present arrangements could not substantially be re-instated.

7. There are, in my view, two significant matters which need to be considered and resolved, and they may be summarised in this way:

(i) Is the proposed Day-Centre/Soup Kitchen an appropriate use for part of a church? And, if it is,

(ii) Is it an appropriate use of this particular Church?

8. So far as the first matter is concerned, I have no doubt, in my mind, that this is a wholly proper use. It seems to me that the Christian mission would have little meaning unless it were prepared to provide *(inter alia)* for such people as are likely to make use of the Day Centre.

9. The second matter is undoubtedly more difficult. I am satisfied that there is a need in Central Exeter for the intended purposes of this Day Centre. But is this an appropriate place in which to provide them? It is said that the arrangement will increase the number of travellers in this area, and that since their activities are unattractive to many people, this will adversely affect trade and tourism in the immediate vicinity of the Church. I can fully understand the anxiety which has been expressed by the objectors and by others who are worried by the proposals.

10. Nevertheless in my judgment the fears which have been expressed are probably exaggerated. I very much doubt whether the proposals will have the adverse effect which some anticipate.

11. In these circumstances I propose to grant the Faculty which has been

sought.

12. In the course of consultation, a number of points have been raised by various bodies (including the Central Council for the Care of Churches and by English Heritage). These matters have been considered by the petitioners, and I am satisfied that the petitioners either have dealt or intend to deal with them in a responsible manner.

13. The petitioners have made it plain that they may wish to dispose of some pews and the organ. I have the helpful report of the Organ Adviser to the Diocesan Advisory Committee, and I accept that report. It does not seem to me that the issue of a Faculty need be held up whilst it is decided how these items should be dealt with. I shall reserve these two particular matters. If the petitioners wish to dispose of these items, and so to alienate them from the Church, then before that is done I must be consulted and my approval obtained to what is proposed.

14. So far as costs are concerned, it seems to me that the objections that were raised were reasonable, and that they were presented in a reasonable manner. I am minded to order that the petitioners should themselves bear the cost of obtaining the Faculty, but that otherwise there should be no order as to costs. If either the petitioners or the objectors wish to contend otherwise, then, obviously, I will be prepared to consider such submissions as they would wish to make. I would only express the hope that these submissions could be put into writing and dealt with without the necessity of a hearing in open court.

David Calcutt
Sir David Calcutt
6 May 1994

APPENDIX THREE: EXETER COMMUNITY UMBRELLA

As the work of the Palace Gate Project developed, different branches were beginning to grow. The variety was a source of encouragement but this also represented a potential problem. Should the Project itself retain control of every new venture that might be started? Apart from other considerations, it would be difficult to supply both the management and the expertise required. So the policy was to be involved at the outset in the work but once formulated to set up a service that would be semi-autonomous under a parent organisation.

The Project team spoke to a number of people in the field of legal and charitable expertise. Very quickly, the idea of the Exeter Community Umbrella (ECU) was born. It was recognised that the need for charitable status was important. It was further recognised at this early stage that ECU needed to be bigger than the Palace Gate Project and to allow other valuable pieces of community work going on in the city to take advantage of its structure.

The decision to set up a charitable limited company was essentially because the management committees of the services provided were better equipped for the grassroots work of providing care than for administering the bureaucratic and legal requirements which were increasingly demanded of the voluntary sector. Secondly, and linked to this, was the advent of a new Charities Act which had tightened up the administration of charities and increased the responsibilities of trustees. Because the Exeter Community Umbrella is a registered charitable trust (Registered Charity No. 1026229) the individual projects would not be burdened with the need to seek individual charitable status and donors can send gifts to ECU to be used as they stipulate.

This has resulted in people being able to devote more of their time to the project work they are really concerned with, while ECU carries part of the administrative load by being the legal employers of all members of staff, dealing with the Inland Revenue and the Department of Social Security, handling insurance, leases, contracts with statutory services and others, and auditing the accounts.

The Exeter Community Umbrella Ltd comprises a variety of people from local churches and the wider community, working closely with representatives of statutory organisations, filling an expert and helpful role of enabling those engaged in charitable work locally by reducing day to day concerns over matters that can sometimes seem a mystery to the non-legal mind!

An important feature of ECU is that it is big enough to embrace more projects in the years ahead so that good ideas, rooted in the community, will be able to come to fruition in a way that would otherwise be impossible. Sadly, many good schemes are never realised simply because the people with the vision lack the experience or the know-how required to set up an effective committee, or to apply for charitable status or even to raise the money (possibly several hundred pounds) to support such an application.

Currently, the Exeter Community Umbrella looks after four projects: Palace Gate Project, St Petrock's Day Centre, Turntable Furniture Project and the Exeter Homes Committee.

Aims and objectives

The objectives of the Exeter Community Umbrella Ltd are listed in its Memorandum and Articles of Association:

> '(i) To promote the benefit of the inhabitants of the City of Exeter and neighbourhood in the County of Devon without distinction of sex or of any political or religious or other opinions, to provide facilities in the interests of social welfare for recreation and for leisure time occupations with the objects

of improving the conditions of life for the said inhabitants;

(ii) To relieve people who are in need, particularly persons who are homeless or threatened with homelessness.'

A separate mission statement explains the aims of ECU:

'We are a charitable organisation registered with the Charity Commissioners. Supported by mainstream Christian denominations, we are motivated by the desire to follow the Christian principle of care for those in need. 'Our objective is to work with those in need as result of homelessness, unemployment, loneliness or lack of appropriate support.

'We seek to complement existing services and provision, by offering practical help and emotional support to lead to increased self-esteem and dignity.

'Our approach is:
- to empower people to achieve their potential
- to operate in an open and business-like manner
- to make realistic provision
- to avoid unfair discrimination and to promote an equal opportunity policy
- to employ staff with attention to fairness, welfare, health and safety
- to raise awareness of our objectives in such a way that funding is obtained by projects and then responsibly managed.'

APPENDIX FOUR: ADDRESSES

For more information on the Exeter Community Umbrella Ltd please contact:

    The Secretary

    Exeter Community Umbrella Ltd

    Westhay

    Streatham Rise

    Exeter EX4 4PE

    Tel: 01392 73525

For more information on the St Petrock's Day Centre please contact:

    St Petrock's Day Centre

    10 Cathedral Yard

    Exeter EX1 1HJ

    Tel: 01392 422396

For more information on the Turntable Furniture Project please contact:

    Turntable Furniture Project

    Units 5 & 6, Exeter City Council Recycling Park

    Tan Lane

    Exton Road

    Marsh Barton Trading Estate

    Exeter EX2 8LX

    Tel: 01392 499477

For more information on all other services please contact:

    Palace Gate Project

    3 Palace Gate

    Exeter EX1 1JA

    Tel: 01392 493123